Mama C

I was not to meet you at Global Citizen NOW as it was my first time!

Praise for *Finding Purpose*

'I've known Thami for a few years and had no idea of the power that sits behind this consummate professional who is truly living her purpose. I read her book in one sitting because I was so engrossed and inspired by her journey. She is the epitome of when the time is right for you, you will be ready and take your crown. I absolutely love the idea of taking your skeletons out of the closet and burying them. That's what holds a lot of us back. This book reminded me that no matter your previous circumstances, when you lean into what was meant for you, you have no choice but to flourish. Thank you Thami for writing a book that is a testimony to that!

– KHENSANI NOBANDA

I was hoping to get this book to you personally!

I LOVE YOU
and I wanted you to know.

Regards
Thami Ntadimeng   (+27762735262)
So South, Africa.

FINDING PURPOSE

LESSONS FROM
THE MESSAGE ARCHITECT

Thami Nkadimeng

KWELA BOOKS

Kwela Books,
an imprint of NB Publishers, a division of Media24 Boeke (Pty) Ltd
40 Heerengracht, Cape Town, South Africa
PO Box 879, Cape Town 8000, South Africa
www.kwela.com

Copyright © Text: Thami Nkadimeng 2024
Copyright © Published edition Kwela Books 2024

All rights reserved.
No part of this book may be reproduced or transmitted in any form
or by any electronic or mechanical means, including photocopying
and recording, or by any other information storage or retrieval system,
without written permission from the publisher.

Cover design: Wilna Combrinck
Cover image: Benedict Jimu
Typography: Marthie Steenkamp
Editor: Tracey Hawthorne
Proof reader: Angela Voges

Set in 12pt on 15 pt Proforma
Printed and bound by CTP Printers, Cape Town

First published by Kwela Books 2024

ISBN: 978-0-7957-1094-0
ISBN: 978-0-7957-1095-7 (epub)

Contents

Foreword by Lincoln Mali		7
Introduction		13
1.	The irony of authentic living	17
2.	A dis-ordered life	29
3.	Every experience contributes to the masterpiece	45
4.	Embrace life's promises	61
5.	When your inner voice speaks, listen	73
6.	My two little lifesavers	87
7.	Who are you?	97
8.	Be truthful to yourself	113
9.	What's love got to do with it?	125
10.	Crossing boundaries in life's journey	137
11.	I'm a bestselling book in life's library and so are you	149
12.	Uncover the journey of your destiny	161
13.	Give and take	173
Conclusion		183
Acknowledgements		187
About the author		189

Foreword

I come from a generation of storytellers. To master their craft, storytellers have to be passionate about other people's stories. Listening to each story broadens our knowledge and makes us better storytellers. I'm always listening to such stories, and I'm inspired by their uniqueness and authenticity.

A couple of years back, I participated in an online conference with Thami Nkadimeng as the moderator. I was highly impressed with her work, and we agreed that we would work together again. I was amazed by her attention to detail, her business acumen and her uncanny ability to knit together different strands of thought into coherent themes for the audience.

Since that conference, her career has skyrocketed to global heights. She is now one of the most promising leaders across the African continent. She has worked, and continues to work, with presidents, leaders, executives, corporates and organisations worldwide. Her crowning achievement – thus far – has been to be named on the '100 Under 40' list of the Most Influential People of African Descent (MIPAD) in support of the International Decade for People of African Descent proclaimed by the United Nations General Assembly.

I received a call one day, and Thami was on the line, and she asked me about my publishing journey, and informed me that she plans to write and publish her book within a specified timeframe. She further told me that she would want me to do the foreword to a book that had not been written – but I later found out that this was the authentic indefatigable Thami Nkadimeng. Thami is a force of nature: once her mind is set, very little can dissuade her. I had to adjust my timeframe to be in line with her burning desire to publish this book her way and in her timeframe.

Hers is a remarkable and inspirational story. Thami as a child always wanted to entertain all the guests at her home by reading a poem or busting a dance move – 'anything to make people listen and pay attention, even if for just a few minutes'. She describes herself as that young girl with pigtails, with high hopes for a bright future. She takes us on her childhood journey that was characterised by a love for languages and drama. She felt that drama helped her come out of her shell a little more authentically.

As she grew up, what she loved and wanted became clearer: 'I had found what I loved doing in essence – languages and drama, and bringing people together – and the other subjects felt like a waste of time to me. I had no idea how I would use these three aspects together in the future, but they were my love and made my heart happy.'

As Thami continued her work, she realised that she was a builder – an architect. She felt that this was her calling: 'I build with my wisdom, my voice and my experience. I architect messages and conversations that impact humanity positively, whether it be through corporate contributions to humanity or on subjects that affect us all globally as people, humans and society.'

Here was a young girl, born in Soweto, a loving and supportive mum on her side, a loving husband, a beautiful family with her two sons that she absolutely adores, and a demanding professional schedule – the world was her oyster. This was the kind of story people wanted to hear, it was the 'perfect script'.

But then Thami then goes on to spoil this 'perfect script', and she eloquently explains her reasons: 'If you want to make any form of impact, you need to expose yourself to other humans, and humans come filled with opinions, and those opinions are sometimes not positive nor dressed fairly or appropriately when dished out.'

She decided to take a bold and courageous approach, to find a way to be comfortable with some of the things that were 'not so cute' about her life, 'because if I have unpacked them, there is absolutely nothing uncomfortable about them being discussed by others on my behalf. If others speak about my past, for example, I have the power to provide details to the story, as I was there, making those mistakes myself, but I can only fully do that if I am comfortable with opening my own closet to reveal the skeletons.'

She took this approach because she strongly believes that the experiences she has gone through could serve as lessons, motivators and warnings for others.

In key moments, when Thami's words are clearly directed at individual readers, she says, 'Learning to be strong – to be an assertive woman – has been a road indeed for me. That road has had both tarred and gravel surfaces, as well as the sharpest turns and, at times, the smoothest lines. It is a road that has given me perspective.' She cautions all of us who expect a perfect life with key time milestones that life doesn't always play out that way. And she gives us a sense of her reality: 'The universe gave me an opportunity to break the template of a "perfect life" in many ways, and for this I am beyond thankful.'

This is the essence of Thami's book. If you only focus on the specific hardships or painful episodes she has shared about her life for a narrow and superficial 'mgosi' about a public figure, then this book is not for you. This book is about someone sharing deeply and openly about some life lessons she has learned, and a generous gift of items in the toolbox of how she became the woman and professional she is today.

In this book, she is, she says, 'fully Thami'. 'I have not written it so you can feel pity for me, as I have already lived these moments and made it out of them. Rather, I am sharing parts of my story with you to encourage the next individual and to show that, no matter how bad things may seem, there is always a way out. I have faced my thunderstorms, and now I am happy to display my rainbows: to demonstrate my teachings through my work, my personality and experiences thus far. My journey is far from over but if I look at the weather forecast of my life, I believe it is going to be mostly sunny, with a few showers here and there, rather than thunderstorms all the way through.'

She proudly asserts, 'I am not perfect, and I do not ever want to be perfect, because that would mean I have nothing further to learn. I want life to keep teaching me ... I want to continue scripting and rehearsing, to continue performing and to continue reviewing, because that is the only way to confidently say that I honestly gave it my best shot to live, and not just to exist.'

Each one of us has a story, and in this book Thami proudly owns her past, her present and her future. This book is about her story and her journey through her eyes and her words, and in that way, she gives power to others to own their stories.

Thami leaves her readers with lots to ponder about their sense of identity, purpose in life and how they embrace their past. She challenges us to be our sometimes flawed yet authentic selves instead of wearing the perfect masks for societal approval.

I'm sure we'll hear more about Thami as she architects messages within South Africa and throughout the world!

Lincoln Mali
October 2023

Introduction

I never seriously thought that I would be an author, although I did 'speak it into life' in 2017. In the process of putting this book together, I went through my social media page and realised that it was in 2017 when my life started to feel like my life, and I felt comfortable in my skin; it was then that I wrote that one day I would pen parts of my story. I wasn't sure if I would do this in the form of a memoir or not, but I was certain that I would write about my life experiences one day. Now, as I write this book, I have two years to go before I turn forty; and by the time it is published, it will be the curtain call to my thirties, and the beautiful giant leap into the years when apparently life is actually 'meant to begin'. Well, judging by my life, living began a whole lot sooner!

I believe that the experiences I have gone through could serve as lessons, motivators and warnings for others. I have always wanted my life lessons not to be wasted – to be lessons for others. For me, what is the point of going through some of the most difficult of life challenges, only for them to be memories? I need them to be memories with a cause.

This book shares some life lessons I have learned, and items in the toolbox of how I became The Message Architect. In this book, I am fully Thami. I have not written it so you can feel pity for me, as I have already lived these moments and made it out of them. Rather, I am sharing parts of my story with you to encourage the next individual and to show that, no matter how bad things may seem, there is always a way out. (Feel free to insert your own life challenges at the various spots where it feels right and correct to do so!)

This book is no way a memoir – I still have way too much life to live, and I have just begun the expansion phase. It's not an autobiography either – so while the stories will help you to get to know me better, they are only threads in the knitting process, and not my entire blanket of life thus far.

Because we all experience life differently and yet also similarly, this is also a book that is possibly a lightbulb that can be switched on by those who are still in a dark phase of their life. We're all in the same storm but in different boats – some are on yachts while others are in canoes. But we're all going to make it to the other side eventually!

Remember that nobody on this earth has a manual for how to live life – none of us has lived it before, we may have guides but certainly not manuals. It is all trial and error. We are all just trying our best, and we will all experience both wins and losses throughout the journey.

I believe that when the message is needed enough, the platforms will avail themselves. This applies not just to my life; it has been my experience testimony after testimony as the years have passed. Lessons present themselves to us from the beginning of our lives and throughout our existence; how quickly we learn from them determines how quickly we evolve to the next level of ourselves.

This book is a gift from me to the world, a token of appreciation for the lessons I've learned thus far. And it is an indicator that your story, too, is important and required, and so it must be heard.

Happy reading and mostly happy reflecting!

Thami Nkadimeng
New York, September 2023

1

The irony of authentic living

If you know me, you know that the very basis of my communication style is to simplify the method of communication and the words used to make sure that everyone understands what is being said.

Let's start with the words I could not find alternatives for but which have a great ring to them. What is irony? It is the juxtaposition of what on the surface appears to be the case, on the one hand, and what the case actually is (or is to be expected), on the other. And what is authenticity? Authenticity is being genuine, and sticking to the real side of yourself with clarity; it means living your life according to your own needs and values, rather than those that society, friends and family expect from you.

The very concept of striving for authenticity in this world is ironic, because we are told to be ourselves, on the one hand, but in the same breath we are told to conform to society's standards, on the other. What if your individual authenticity is not to fit in but rather to be the one who kicks the imaginary box to the side?

So the question is: can we truly live authentically in today's world?

Life being unsolvable in itself, it would be a mystery if it did not contain all sorts of contradictions. I face and watch all kinds of these on a daily basis. We drive around in a leafy suburb where we see people hungry and begging for food. We live in a world where people are fighting for peace, and are shot at peaceful protests, to mention a few.

Contradiction is part of discovery. If we did not have fluidity in life, it would mean that life would be fixed and rigid, and that would rule out the option of choice, of making up our own minds and creating our own opportunities.

I no longer fear life's templates. I am happy to live an authentic life even though it also comes with contradictions that could be considered ironic. I am happy to fight for justice while the journey serves me injustice, or to fight for magnificence while I allow myself to make life mistakes during discovery. It gives me the choice to go with the flow or to swim upstream, in accordance with my desired results.

Youth is the time in our lives when we learn about ourselves. I spent mine trying to 'unlearn' my innate qualities so that I could build qualities that could accommodate the circumstances I was in and help me survive. My life brought me chaos in order to ultimately bring me order, and so I found myself only learning about my innate self much later on in life.

I started sharing intimate parts about my life publicly through my first TEDx talk, which I delivered in 2022. I had thought that I would share my life at a much later stage but I was too 'in my flow' when it happened to not trust the process.

I was nominated in 2021 to deliver that TEDx talk by someone who had watched me moderate a number of public conversations. Moderating public conversations involves being a neutral member of a debate or discussion, helping to define the aims of the discussion, and clarifying its outcomes – I do this on television, during live coverage for conferences on news channels around the world, and on stage, for example, when I hosted the South African Investment Conference and moderated in the United Nations General Assembly. The person who nominated me for the talk had been on the planning team for a conference on which I was lead moderator, and she had also watched me programme-direct a few events, which involves curating the narrative of the event and weaving speakers together to ensure that delegates leave the room having been delivered content in a manner that is consumable. She thought I would be perfect for the challenge of telling the story about how I became a success in the field of moderating panel discussions, and a television host.

TED Talks, the first of which were delivered in 2006, were an offshoot of TED, a non-profit, non-partisan organisation that aims to 'create a future worth pursuing for all'. TED began in 1984 as a conference where technology, entertainment and design converged.

TEDx events are local gatherings where live TED-like talks and performances are shared with the community. The content and design of each TEDx event is unique and developed independently, consisting of a suite of short, carefully prepared talks, demonstrations and performances that are idea-focused, and cover a wide range of subjects to foster learning and inspiration, and provoke conversations that matter.

The talk series in which I was invited to participate, part of TEDxlytteltonWomen, was showcasing speakers from around the continent who represent women's political, economic and civic participation under the theme 'What now?' I accepted the challenge – but I didn't know it would be the eye-opening experience of my life!

(Proving that what is meant to be, will always be, I had actually applied to be a TEDx speaker in 2019, but that did not work out, as I had tonsillitis on the day of the auditions, and this affected my delivery. So I packed away that prayer and did not visit it again. We may forget our prayers, but once they are out there, they are out there!)

I was given three months to plan for the 2022 talk, and assigned a coach to guide me in the process and advise me according to previous talks they had listened to or studied. (I met up virtually with my coach and to this day have not met him in real life!)

It was a super-busy time for me. I had to prepare for the talk in between working and travelling. In my work, I programme-direct and moderate global and African conversations, and at the time I was preparing for events such Uniting to Combat Neglected Tropical Diseases with Heads of States and FAME Week Africa, during which African and global creative professionals gather for content sessions, music showcases, film screenings, exhibitions and a variety of networking opportunities. I was also still a full-time employee at the time. Preparing for my TEDx talk was to take place in the middle of this busy schedule, which felt like a complete whirlwind. Still, I obviously gave the preparation for it my utmost attention.

I decided to structure my talk around the few months of work I had done in 2019 with the American author of four bestselling books on human and brand behaviour, Timothy Maurice Webster. At the time I was working as a communications executive for a company in the mining and sustainable building industry, and I had just finished my maternity leave after having given birth to my second child. I needed to make a solid decision for the future. I had decided I wanted to be a global moderator, navigating conversations and panels for leaders around the world to find direction and outcomes that will benefit humanity and society.

When I decide to do something, I plan as fully as possible for it. This is why I made contact with Tim – I wanted us to have a few sessions mapping out the direction I could possibly take to define my place in the market and the impact I wanted to make through this career for the world. Those a few sessions became months of us unpacking my story in depth.

After he had listened me narrate my life story to him, Tim suggested that while my life was like a drama, we could not call me a 'drama queen' because that would have negative connotations. So perhaps a better way of saying it, he suggested, was that my life was like theatre. This created a backbone of a structure which entailed scripting, rehearsals, performance and reviews in line with the theatre theme.

Come dress-rehearsal day, 48 hours before the delivery of the actual talk, the coaches and organisers told me that I sounded angry, insincere and inauthentic in my delivery. Well, they were correct: I *was* angry. I was mad that I had so much to say but did not have the courage to say it, because

I was afraid of how the world might judge me as the public figure I was becoming in my new career of moderating.

In order for you to understand this fear of mine, you need to know that I had come into the moderating and programme-directing industry like a wrecking ball (this is actually how I was described by some people) – I wanted to ensure that I made way not only for my own breakthroughs but for others too, by breaking down the walls. I had been told in no uncertain terms that the moderating space was reserved by industry leaders for qualified journalists, and I was in no way a qualified journalist. What I did have, however, were natural journalism strengths and qualities, an intensive communication background and the tertiary education to back that up. Still, anyone who speaks in and to the public is really open to scrutiny – and judgement. So being 'perfect' seemed like the only way to keep my space in the moderating arena.

With this at the forefront of my mind, I did not want to cause what felt like too much more chaos on the speaking circuit, and for this reason I felt I needed to project myself as being perfect in every sense to be accepted. I thought that sharing my childhood story through my TEDx talk would potentially taint this 'pretty' (if inaccurate) image we are encouraged to share as public figures. But how else could I advance on the public-speaking circuit if I didn't share with my audience who I really am?

When I got off that stage after the disastrous rehearsal, I cried; not just cried, but ugly-cried. I made three separate phonecalls: one to my husband, one to my friend and one to my mom. I told my husband, Tony, that the next 48 hours were going to be tough, because it was time for me to fully grow into my own skin. I told my friend, Lefentse Makoko, how scared I was to open up to the world about who I am. And I asked my mother, Johanna, for her permission to tell my story, because I could not tell my story without telling parts of hers. She was hesitant at first but ultimately said that she trusted me to do it with dignity.

I drove to the office (I was still a full-time employee with the same company) for a meeting that could have happened virtually, but for which I am glad I went in physically, because it was the start of my life taking shape. The corporate world can be a jungle, a game of *Survivor* where everyone must outwit, outplay and outlast each other in every sense. Everyone knows they're playing the game but nobody talks about it.

As soon as that meeting wrapped up, I went back home to what awaited me: the difficult task of getting real with myself. My carefully structured and memorised talk had to change – not a little but practically the entire thing.

I thought the process would be difficult but it was not. In actual fact, it all came to me so naturally: I was finally going to be let down my guard, so there would be no need to memorise the talk. I would speak from the heart, from a few jotted-down key points.

A day and half later, I poured my heart out on that stage in Centurion, Tshwane, delivering my talk, 'I Used

My Mind's Theatre to Become'. I was sure of one thing: I was going to use this opportunity to the best of my ability. Vulnerable but determined, I spoke for fifteen and a half minutes with a shaking leg.

That talk helped me figure out who I am. It also made me fully embrace that I could not become the best version of myself if I did not acknowledge where I come from. I am who I am partly because of the contributions of my past. Regardless of how good, bad or ugly it was, my past has shaped me in one way or the other. I am thankful for it. I love my past, my present and my future. All in all, I love my life and I am glad it was assigned to me to live it, and I will live it fully.

Little did I know that that would only be the beginning of this backbone growing, and that there was still such a journey and a rollercoaster to ride.

Unlike in actual theatre, where there is a beginning and an end to the show, our lives' starting and ending times are not pre-advertised. But our lives' theatre is still theatre, a show that must be played out and watched. We may not be able to re-take scenes but they can be rescripted in any way you want them to be. *You* are the only main character in this show called life, and the other characters you can write in and write out as and when you please, or when the mortal life decides – some you may want to have in your life for life, but death takes them away.

In my life, the only main characters in my story besides myself are my mom, my husband and my two sons. They are the 'starrings', as we would say when we were growing up – and we pronounced the word 'steering', meaning that those people play a very important part in this theatre.

Perhaps, having read this chapter, you will realise that the very authenticity that makes me was the irony I had been living. The very darkness that was meant to break me was the darkness that built me. A large portion of my life up until now has been contradictory in many ways; however, put together, it is the definition of my authenticity.

The fact that I have been given the opportunity to create a truth out of the contradictions of my life, and to make sense of it to myself and the world, is a gift. Some people are given darkness and struggle to find the sense in it all, and I do not take it for granted that I jumped at the very first sign of light I was able to fathom and make out.

All of us have areas in our lives that make absolutely no sense to others – and they do not need to, because they are there to teach each of us individual lessons. Although these unique areas may be considered contradictions to others, they are portions that make up *your* story and they are authentic to *you*. Your true self is found not only in the linear parts of life that seem straight and clean; it is also found in the mess of it all.

The conflict with society's demands and requirements is often where the 'realness' of each person lies, because we have to dig deep to keep our authenticity in a world that requires that we be what others want us to be. If we were all always in agreement, would there ever be authenticity for us as unique people; and, even more so, if we were all always in agreement, would the irony of life then not lie in all of us contradicting ourselves and our beliefs to conform?

We are all a bunch of contradictions walking around authentically, and that is the beauty of life. Yes, what society demands of us, and our own authenticity, must live side by side if our lives are to grow to their full potential. If we do not allow this full potential, we stifle the growth, and then we will never realise what we could all ultimately be in our fullness.

Life is ultimately energy strung together in every moment; even how we are physically pieced together is energy pieced together, I believe – it took energy to create each one of us. If we do not allow our full potential to flourish through authenticity, we shock and stress the energy of life. Have you ever seen a shocked animal or human, or even a stressed plant? They either shrivel up, or remain stuck in a position without the ability to move on to the next opportunity, and as a result become only a fraction of what they possibly could have become. Tap into your emotions, and remember that even if your truth seems ironic to the next person, it does not make your 'realness' untrue.

Stop judging yourself if your life does not unfold or proceed according to societal norms. You are a normal part of the pot of life's deliciousness, and so is everyone else.

> To be authentic often requires going against societal norms.

2

A dis-ordered life

I've come to realise that life is a delicious meal, eaten backwards by some people and in the conventional order by others. I say this because in universal merit, dessert is the best part of any coursed meal. This is because it's the sweet part, the indulgent part.

If life were a standard three-course meal, I'm almost certain that my life from birth to my thirties was the main course. Yes, it did contain a whole lot of lemon and bucketloads of cayenne pepper, but it sure did feed me and is enabling me to have sustenance for life!

I'm currently on my starter course. The appetiser is an important part of any meal: it sets you up for the rest of the consumption, and different components of it may be served separately, but can certainly be enjoyed together. What I am currently experiencing in my thirties is exactly that: serving and offering different parts of me to the world in the roles I play in my family and society separately and together, but they are the most important parts of me, the largest parts of me. If my imagination serves me – and it has never failed me yet! – then this part of my life's meal will last until I'm in my sixties, after which I'll jump into dessert.

A sequence is a set of related events, movements or items that follow each other in a particular order. But who determines the order of the sequence, especially when it comes to how our lives unfold? Why does society emphasise that we must be born, grow up, go to university, build a career, find a life partner and then have children? I do believe if this was meant to be the order of a perfect life, then we would have been made in a factory to reduce any opportunity faults!

An example is that I rushed into my first marriage in my mid-twenties because society says we are supposed to get married in that age period, right? Wrong! You should get married when the time is right – when you have the right partner who you have asked all the correct questions to make sure you are aligned on how to handle potential situations that you may both come across. That was a big step I missed before getting into my first marriage and I paid a heavy price for it, figuratively and literally.

If I reflect on my life, none of it has been in what our society may consider to be sequential order, but I am happy with it. In fact, it's the very reason I am happy where I am today. So, although I describe my life as being in mains–starter–dessert order, it's okay for you to view yours in a different order – dessert–mains–starter or even mains–dessert–starter.

I grew up, from birth to around 10 years of age, in the 'northern suburbs' of Soweto, if you could call it that – an area of Soweto that was considered high-end. Most homes in Soweto back then were big enough to live in but small enough to mass them in a row of streets; these standard-sized houses had a kitchen, lounge, two bedrooms and a bathroom. Our home, however, had in addition a dining area, a long passage and an additional bedroom. We even had a carport, an automated garage and an intercom system at the gate.

This was huge improvement on where my mom, Johanna, came from. She grew up in the village of Seabe, on the border between Limpopo and Mpumalanga provinces. She was number three in a family of seven children. Her mother – my grandmother – was employed as a housekeeper to an incredible family (who I had the honour of also growing close to in my childhood) and her father – my grandfather – was a security guard, so there were no luxuries in my mom's upbringing but they coped with what they had.

My mother is a massive and important part of my story. She has been my motivation to do better in life, even when one step ahead seemed impossible. She is a knowledgeable and expert corporate woman, and an even more sophisticated and veteran businesswoman.

My mother loved school – she was a top student throughout her school life – and she still loves learning. She knew that a good education was the key to a better life, so to make sure she could make it to school every day, she had to teach herself to get used to a pricking pain in her feet – she had no school shoes to wear, and had to walk on thorny sand to and from school. She finally walked the difficult route so often that she no longer felt the pain.

Given this, she always made sure that I had school shoes, and long before I had children – when I was very young – she asked me to please make sure that her grandchildren had two pairs of school shoes each (she knew I would want to have children). And she asked me to ask the same of my own children, so the trajectory of growth for future generations would never find an opportunity to reverse.

What my mother was teaching me at that early age was that each generation had a responsibility to pave the way for the next. She imparted her wisdom to me by being an example of how I can create sustainable generational growth through my choices throughout life.

We had a landline at home, and from when I was very young, every time it rang, I would pick up it up and answer it with precision – 'Thami speaking. Good day. How can I help you?' – as if I was a call-centre agent. My mom's friends would marvel at this, telling her that she must make the best of my language command and smarts.

My mom knew very early on that I had a special relationship with reading and languages, and she wanted to do whatever she could to polish that love. She initially enrolled me in a school that she felt would be beneficial for me because it was outside the township and so would surely help me in fine-tuning my natural skill sets.

That quickly changed when she began realising that, despite my schooling, I was not developing the ability to string sentences together that made sense. She wanted me to be in a school that would help enhance my language skills, as she knew that I would land up in a career that would require linguistics (and she was correct!). So she took me out of that school and placed me in a new one – a private all-girls school in Rosebank.

My mother certainly did not live her life in societal sequence; her life meal was not in what most people would consider normal order. I think my mom's order of life is more mains–starter–dessert. Mom has long passed her half-century mark and she is about to start her dessert era. This makes my heart smile, and I pray that her dessert lasts her into her nineties and beyond.

My mother always looked great. She had a huge Afro, and she loved to wear very high heels and shift dresses to work. I often tease her that she must have given me the ability to walk in heels, because I can walk in any pair of heels with confidence.

Making people happy and serving them was something my mother instilled in me at the core. On Saturdays, Mommy would always bake queen's cakes (cupcake-like confectionery), in case anybody knocked at our door. She did this to make sure that visitors would have something delicious to eat.

I was the child who always wanted to entertain all the guests at home by reading a poem or busting a dance move – anything to make people listen and pay attention, even if for just a few minutes.

So – a young girl with pigtails, with high hopes of a bright future, and her ambitious, clever, beautiful mom sounds almost too good to be true, right? Well, it was. Because in our home, we were dealing with trauma and abuse. My father, who was an alcoholic, physically and emotionally abused my mother; and when she wasn't actually getting beaten up by him, he was threatening to beat her up.

My father would become some kind of superman in his mind when he'd had one too many, which gave him the courage to hurt, physically, emotionally and verbally, the people he was meant to love and protect the most. And the more he drank, the more abusive he would become.

I often wonder how that chemical change occurs in the brain of someone who is controlled by alcohol. Do they still see the same human as they are abusing them, or do they see an image of something or someone else? I wonder if this change is gradual or if it happens over a period of time. I wonder if the alcohol only brings out bottled resentment or if it only gives people the courage to do what they would in a sober state but did not have the guts to do?

In 1993, when I was eight years old, one Sunday night my mom, my brother (who was a toddler at the time), my nanny Manie and I moved out in the middle of the night. A big truck came and packed up all the stuff my mom thought we needed to take with us. We jumped into Mommy's Opel Kadett; it was white, with a blue band.

The day she got that car, she was so proud, and I was so proud of her. She had done something major for herself. She had worked hard to afford it, and buying the car meant she could claim her independence. I cannot fault Mommy on this: she taught me to be independent from a very young age, to stand on my own two feet and to save money, to always have backup money available to get myself whatever is required.

For a period of time my dad would take her to a piece of open land near our home to try to teach her how to drive, but then they would fight and it would be chaos. At some point she decided to pay a driving school to teach her, and she finally got her driver's licence.

The night we moved out of our home in Soweto, we followed the truck in the dark. As it trundled along the road in front of us, some of our belongings came loose and fell off. Of course, Mommy stopped to pick them up – she would never have allowed her continental pillows to be lost in that manner!

The journey to Palm Springs, a township between Orange Farm and Sebokeng where my mom's parents (my maternal grandparents) lived, was about forty-five minutes away, but on this particular night it felt like it took forever, probably because of the combination of excitement and anxiety about what lay ahead that I was feeling. I was looking forward to being reunited with my twin cousins (Nthabs and Thabs, who are the same age as me), who lived with our grandparents, and it was one of the reasons I always wanted to be shipped off there during the school holidays. This was going to be an adventure of note!

Of course, I had not thought about what this meant for my schooling or living conditions, because I was a child. I suppose that in my mind I had painted a picture of it as a continuous version of the weekend and holiday visits I spent there. I am glad, however, that this all happened when I was young – I know that when I found out the details later, it stung, so I am not sure my nine-year-old self would have coped with it all.

We arrived and were welcomed with open arms by my grandparents. I ran to the space I would be sharing with the other children. They asked me why we were visiting so late, and I explained that we were not visiting but that I was actually going to live with them for ever and ever. We laughed and started to jump on the bed in excitement.

That was shortlived because Manie – my nanny of fifteen years, from when I was five until I was twenty; my other mom, my partner in . . . shhhhhhh, no need to share those details in this book – came to tell us to go to sleep because we had school the next day.

My mom thought her parents' home would be the safest place for us all to be while she found her feet and tried to carry on with life without my father. My grandparents' house had three bedrooms, a TV room, a kitchen and a bathroom. That may sound like a fairly generous space, but bear in mind that it was shared by ten people at any given time (and when every other member came to visit, that number could rise to fifteen, even twenty).

As you might guess, growing up in this kind of environment had its good times and bad, its pros and cons. Because of the abuse my mother, my brother and I had endured from my father, I was happy in Palm Springs to start with. I was relieved: the weight had been taken off my nine-year-old body and soul, and I knew we were now safe. I loved the laughs, the never being physically lonely because there was always someone there, and the feeling of community.

I lived with two of the coolest and strangest uncles, who also lived with my grandparents at the time. They would fight to the ends of the earth for me but their value systems were questionable. For example, on the one hand, I was not allowed to hang around with a boy at the corner of the street, but on the other, I would be asked to take a cigarette and light it at the heater because they did not have matches on them.

This is how I began smoking, by the way. After so many times of being sent to just light this white and brown object, I thought to act like one of them and take a drag. Boy, did I cough! But that coughing made me want to master the act without coughing. I do not like to fail, and if my uncles could inhale this thing without coughing, I was going to learn too. It did not take me long to master it either.

But the disadvantages were significant. Sharing a small space which meant minimal privacy, and our lists of chores sometimes seemed endless. Being continuously compared to the other children in the home could be dispiriting – I was compared to my cousins all the time on school work and body shape too. I was sworn at because not all adults have the same conduct and some of them thought cursing would get us to understand them better (I must say I do not think it was intentionally thought out). Sometimes the adults would not take time to understand our childish squabbles and I would land up scolded and getting a hiding for things I actually did not do.

These disadvantages were draining – so draining that some of them took decades to shrug off mentally.

I continued to attend my private all-girls school in Rosebank. My mom didn't move me to a school nearer to my grandparents' home, partly because she sort of wanted to keep some things constant within so much change going on in our lives, but also because, I know now, she was determined to give us the best education at whatever cost.

I had to wake up at four-thirty every morning to make it to school on time. I had to be ready to leave the house by quarter past five-ish, driven by my grandfather, to beat the traffic. I would bath the night before, so in the morning all I had to do was a wipe-down, brush my teeth and shove breakfast down my throat. To this day I struggle to eat breakfast early in the morning; it just does not sit well with my body.

The teachers had to be alerted of my altered life circumstances but none of my fellow learners quite understood what I was dealing with. I would watch the other kids being picked up by their moms and dads in the afternoon as soon as school was out, but I had to wait until around four thirty in the afternoon, when my grandfather arrived to do the return drive. Over time, I started to learn how to fill those afternoons with fun activities with my friends. We would entertain ourselves with games such as general knowledge (where one of us would pick a letter of the alphabet, and then we all had to name an animal, a car, an occupation and an object beginning with that letter).

So the long hours were still long but I did not feel them that much after a while. And, as a result, working long hours now for me is no problem; it is just a way of life that I had to become accustomed to at an early age, a case of 'you gotta do what you gotta do'.

While I felt 'less-than' at school, where I was considered a chubby loudmouth, while the other girls seemed to be perfect, back at home, I was Little Miss Perfect to the other children in the neighbourhood. They were fascinated by how I spoke English, how I articulated my words and could change my accents. They were even more fascinated by the fact that I went to school with children of all races. They would ask me to rattle off a few sentences, and would be left laughing, looking at me with eyes wide open, and trying to explore this wonder that I was. (Some still say I am a wonder today!) I loved the attention, and I loved to make people happy, so I was only too glad to be a source of entertainment for them.

I wasn't the prettiest girl in the neighbourhood. Now, in the township, you would be boxed: there were the 'hot' girls, and then there was often the ultimate girl – the one who was the standard of beauty in that township. If you looked nothing like her, did not have a body shape like hers or did not wear clothes like her, you belonged with the rest of us.

(I wonder why there was never the *smartest* one being pranced around? We really need to work on that as a society going forward – to make education cool and aspirational.)

Once a year there would be a neighbourhood beauty contest, a modelling competition. It was structured in flow like many beauty pageants, so there would be categories such as 'swimsuit', 'evening dress' and 'casual wear'. Now that I was living with my cousin Nthabs, who everyone around believed could become a future Miss South Africa, these kinds of competitions became all too familiar to me, as they were openly discussed in the household.

She would go to rehearsals and would tell me all the interesting stories when she returned. But I wanted to experience it all for myself, so I decided I would attend with her. By simple observation, I learned which clothes the contestants had to pack and how they had to walk on the ramp, and all the twirling and posing spots too. My young brain never understood why the adults around me were willing to pay twenty rands entrance fee for my cousin to be a part of this competition but not me. It was a beauty contest, and I was also beautiful, right?

On the day of the competition, very quietly, I packed the required clothes alongside my cousin, and when we arrived at the competition, I was also ready to compete. I was going to show everyone that I could win because of how beautiful I was. I had no idea what 'chubby' meant in the world; I knew my body was different from my cousin's, but I did not see it as ugly.

I competed with the biggest smile and the happiest heart, and I won Ms Congeniality! I may not have been considered the prettiest girl in room, but I was at the very least the nicest. My prizes were a bottle of lotion and a roll-on deodorant – the first toiletries I ever owned without them being procured for me at my mom's expense.

My floating on cloud nine was shortlived. First, I had not let my mom know I was going to compete, and I now owed the organisers twenty rand. My mom paid it, but I got shouted at, not for participating but for not communicating honestly.

And then – and much more seriously – one of my uncles laughed and asked why I had entered the competition. I was too fat to be participating in beauty contests, he explained.

When I really thought about it, I realised that most of the girls in the contest were indeed slim-figured compared to me, and so I was determined to get slimmer to fit in and be beautiful. That began my struggle with my weight.

Bob Harper, the American fitness specialist and personal trainer who presented *The Biggest Loser*, once said, 'It has to be hard so you will never forget.' He was referring to the weight-loss process and how the experience of losing weight should be so burdensome that the person going through it is motivated not to gain the weight back again.

I told myself that to get thinner, I simply had to stop eating, so that is what I did. It started with having two meals a day, instead of three; then cutting out foods that I felt did not serve me; then it became one meal a day; and finally it became a slice of bread per day. The change in my body was so gradual that it was initially unnoticeable to those around me.

I was eating less but I was also being more active. I loved netball – nothing mattered to me as much as netball. I would have rather failed academically than on the court; never on the court!

So I was getting tinier and tinier by the day, until my bones started to show. I did not care about my health; I was finally achieving that 'beauty' status and standard. I could wear whatever I wanted, and that was the goal.

Of course, that is such a joke – I could have worn whatever I wanted, whatever weight I was. But as someone who didn't like to fail, I was winning at what I wanted to achieve. Who's Ms Congeniality now?

In a typical sequence of life, you really have no idea or care of how you look when you are young and carefree. When, usually around puberty (but often younger), you become super-aware and conscious that your weight defines your beauty, you begin to try and do whatever it needed to look a particular way to please society, whether this is extreme diet plans, extreme surgeries, or both.

But the good news is that I finally reached an age of comfortableness in my late thirties, after having had my second child. I am happy to be in a place now where I love myself and would never consider extreme methods in the name of beauty. These days, I do care not to be overweight for health reasons. Still, these childhood experiences do scar us: today, I do not use the brand of lotion or roll-on that I won in that beauty contest, despite it still being available on the shelves – the smell triggers me and I think of the weight struggle and shame I felt being chubby, so I prefer to stay very far from it.

I am finally happy with knowing that the sequence of events in your life are never meant to mirror those of your friends, colleagues and others. That is the beauty of originality.

> Don't worry if your life sequence doesn't run in an accepted order – it'll all make sense in the end.

3

Every experience contributes to the masterpiece

A puzzle is created as a whole picture first. It is then cut into pieces, and those pieces have to be put back together carefully to create the full picture again. All the pieces play a role, but they all play a different role. And a puzzle can always be pulled apart and pieced together, for its span of durability.

With this analogy in mind, I have come to the conclusion that all our lives already have a bigger picture when we are born. We just need to discover it as we journey along.

As we start to notice the pieces, we collect them. Those who are deliberate may start to put the pieces together sooner, and the picture of their life will become clearer more quickly, even though all the pieces have not been collected yet.

Most puzzles have four corners. When building a puzzle, I usually use the corners as the starting point, then fill in the borders, and finally finish off building the centre of it all.

The corners are fundamental to the whole picture. I would like to take you through one of the 'corner pieces' in life in the hope that you will be encouraged to think deeply and start to discover your own.

I spent my first two years of school, Grades 1 and 2, at a school of which I have very few memories, except an extremely vivid one of the first day, and of the day we had our photos taken for the school magazine. I was short (well, I still am!) and I was put in the front row. Thank goodness as an adult I am able to wear heels!

Due to my shortness, most of the uniform was oversized on me in my early years of school, and Mommy would stuff cotton wool into the toes of my shoes to make them fit. My blazer was another story: the sleeves had to be folded back twice. Yes, my mom did buy the smallest size available in stores and still that required altering because I was swimming in it.

Another memory I have of school was that we would, every once in a while, have a dress-length check: dresses had to be no shorter than three fingers above the knee.

There was no need to worry about my dress not being above my knees in length – it was just about touching my ankles! – until I got to high school, of course.

My last two years of secondary education, from the age of fifteen to seventeen (Grades 11 and Matric), were at an unconventional school that allowed for absolute expression through fashion, hair and even make-up. By then, the dresses I wore were a lot shorter than three fingers above the knee, and I was able to show my gorgeous legs to the world – and, trust me, I did!

For most of my school life, however, I attended an all-girls convent school in Rosebank. (We schoolgirls were not taught to be nuns at the convent school – it was just a normal school. It was the religious belief that was the 'convent' part more than anything. Imagine me as a nun? I think not!)

I've explained a bit about this area of my life because it was my growing-up years, during which school was not 'just school' to me. If you look at the standards of how the smartest children are identified in schools, then you can safely say that I was not the sharpest crayon in the box – but I did still carry out the duty of a crayon, which is to bring colour and flavour through my unique shades. If the definition of 'smart' is having or showing a quick-witted intelligence, and the definition of 'intelligent' is the ability to acquire and apply knowledge and skills, then I guess I was both.

What I am saying is that I never fit in the mould; I actually think I still do not. From a tender age, I figured out the concept of and difference between being book smart, street smart and business savvy, and I was focused on attaining a kind of balance between the three areas rather than on only getting high marks.

Who taught me this?

I used to watch *The Oprah Winfrey Show* carefully and study it – and I mean *study* it. I might have been too young to understand some of the topics of discussion, but what I saw was a woman with an Afro on my television screen who could research and talk about anything she wanted to or was asked to (book smart). I saw a woman who could command the attention of a diverse audience – all races, all ages, all genders, you name it (street smart). And she was – and still is – definitely business savvy.

Only much later did it hit me that I was looking to Oprah for the talents and skill set I was building and would need to hone in my career at a later stage with speaking, conversation and interviewing, and mostly building humanity through talk.

I mentioned crayons and their sharpness. Allow me to ask you this question if you are in a position to influence any children. Why do we pressure children to be the top students in school when we are well aware that all children are gifted differently?

I read a story once that resonated with me when it comes to this point, and I want to paraphrase it for you. If you are a parent or have children around you, or who you care for, or who you influence in any manner, please pay particular attention to this, because it opened my mind to see things differently and from the perspective of a frustrated child. To some degree, I was a frustrated child too in this regard.

School is like having a whole lot of different animals in a classroom, for instance, an elephant, a monkey, a giraffe, a bee, and so on. Imagine that while these animals are in the classroom, we decide to determine their worthiness through a test that will be the same for all of them – the school equivalent of writing exams.

So, the animals open up the test paper, and find what they have to achieve to pass to the next grade. They have to climb a tree, and they will be rated on how fast they can climb it.

This is all good and well for the monkey, and maybe even the bee, but what are we saying to the elephant and giraffe? Does the fact that they can't climb the tree mean that they are useless as animals?

I hope you would join me in encouraging young children to give their own personal, individual best and that is all. Trying to reach percentages that are unattainable is the start of a dislike of learning in one way or the other – I know this because I lived it for most of my young schooling.

Children should be given the opportunity to discover what they love, and hopefully pursue it if encouraged, and motivated to just be *their* best, not *the* best.

The pressures of society start at home, and I am thankful that I grew up with a mom who just asked me to pass, nothing more.

⌒⊃⌒

After having lived with my grandparents for a while, we all moved back in as a family again – Mom, Dad, brother, nanny and me. First, we moved into a white house in Sharonlea, a pretty suburb near Randburg in Johannesburg; a year later, we moved to Sundowner, a few minutes away. The Sundowner house was the home I lived in for the longest, and it was owned by my parents. It resembled our home in Soweto, with a massive back yard. From the outside, it looked like a small compact home, with two separate garages attached to it. In this way, it was a little like myself: small at face value but with huge potential and lots to offer on the inside!

During those years, my parents would collect me after work, and we would then make our way home together once their day at the office was done. Because I knew I was unable to rush home in the afternoons, I filled them up with sports, gossiping in groups and getting up to mischief, as teenagers do – we were too cool to play general knowledge by this stage – anything to avoid doing homework!

I was the biggest nomad in friendship circles at school: I had 'friendly' acquaintances but I never genuinely tried to have deep friendships in high school; I needed to keep a safe distance from the other girls, to prevent them from finding out about the abuse that was continuing to happen at my home. I wanted to be accepted, however, which meant getting just close enough but still keeping everyone secretly at arm's length.

My best friend – we had been besties since we were very young – did not attend the same school as me. I think that not going to the same school helped sustain the friendship – if she had attended the same school, I may have pushed her away. We are still besties now, over thirty years later.

While my drive for women empowerment probably stemmed from watching my mom struggle to be empowered in her home, another factor was that I spent so many of my early years around girls and women, attending an all-girls school where there were women of every shape, colour and size. There were fights and tears (I think there could have been more intentional focus on how we should have been more supportive of each other from that early stage) but there was also love, and first loves, and heartbreaks and gossip, and so much more.

All that said, I lived the most untruthful truth in my school years. What I mean by this is that, truthfully, I was screaming out for help through my antics and actions in so many ways. I was not subtle about it, but we were children, and nobody could ever understand that I was screaming out because home was unbearable. I do wish my teachers had paid more attention; had they paid attention, they would have noticed that all I needed them to do was to care to ask about my home life.

One night, Daddy punched me in my stomach for attending a school fireworks event, and coming home an hour later than I said I would. When he punched me, we were standing in our yard – the place that was my home, the place that I should have been able to run to for safety. He punched me so hard that I could not breathe for a few seconds. I was a confused teenager in a situation I was not equipped to handle; I was not sure whether to cry or to start begging for forgiveness. Nothing would come out of my mouth, anyway: I just stood there, in shock, with my hands on my stomach.

Then, as if nothing had happened, he turned and walked back towards the house, and told me to come inside. It turns out he had had an argument with my mom earlier and I was the perfect stress reliever.

So the 'untruth' was that I used acting as a form of escapism. I felt pressure to come across as perfect because I was compensating for my actual sad reality of a broken home filled with mistreatment. I would create characters and scenarios so I could paint a perfect world that did not exist in real life. I would pretend, for example, that my family and I went on holidays that never really happened. I would create an image of what my home life looked like because nobody knew how I was living or where I stayed – it was a fairy tale of sorts. As a result, I was caught out in lies many times.

Once, when I was in Grade 10, we were in business economics class and I had scored a B for a particular test. I had never scored anything above a D average before in that subject (although I did get to score As in later years, and even got an A average for business economics in Grade 11). My teacher asked me in front of the entire class what had gone right for me to score such a high mark. Many questions immediately flooded my mind: why was she asking me that now, when I'd scored high marks; why had she not asked me what the problem was when I was scoring low marks? Was she trying to make a public mockery of me? Was she asking because she thought she had done a better job of teaching me the subject than teachers in previous terms and years?

So, I answered her with an answer that left her super-uncomfortable: I explained that my dad had moved out of home to go and live elsewhere, and that this had finally given me the time and space to actually study in peace. (Note to all adults: do not ask a child a question if you are not fully ready for a raw and honest answer from them!)

This is how my peers got a glimpse into my actual home life, how they learned that I did not have a perfect life. I found having to share myself in that way uncomfortable; I felt like my privacy had been invaded. Fortunately, nobody asked for any further details and I did not share any further truthful specifics on that situation in a group setting going forward.

Those high school years were my first experiences of trying to impress boys. I was quite a late bloomer physically, and at some point I would tuck socks into my bra for social gatherings (but never at school because I was too afraid that they would fall out or that someone would notice them). I wanted the boys to notice me even if I was considered as having 'rough around the edges' tendencies – I was not into what they call 'girly girl' stuff.

On the weekends, we would ask our parents to drop us off at Sandton City in the evening, and we would roam around the mall, hoping the person we liked was also there. I am not joking – we would literally be dropped off with enough money to buy a meal and maybe pay for a bit of entertainment, and we could sustain our hangout sessions for over six hours, just roaming around the mall – good, clean fun!

At the convent, there was a long balcony, with the classrooms in a row along it. This area had full view of the drop-off and collection area, and you could see all the activity of the cars coming in and driving out. I have distinct memories of rows of girls leaning on that balcony railing to witness whose boyfriend had arrived for a visit and which cute boy was there to drop off a gift for whom.

My school friends and I used to wear our jerseys in the scorching sun. You would not dare to remove that jersey because underneath it was a dress tucked to the shortness of your liking and held up by the belt so that you could show off your legs. If we knew that someone's brother was coming or if there was a boy going to be on the premises, the dresses went up and the jerseys went on.

Our unofficial brother school was St David's Marist, an all-boys school in Inanda. It was an unwritten law among the girls that we all needed to have a boyfriend either from there or from St John's College. There were interschool fireworks nights, raves and parties (called socials).

We figured out how to send letters to each other from one school to the other: the children who caught the school transport that went between the schools, dropping off and collecting kids, became our messengers. These were mostly children from township areas who went to schools in the suburbs, and whose parents had clubbed together and paid a driver in his own transport to take the children to and from school. In this way, love letters were exchanged, passed through the windows at the relevant school.

Those love letters were quite the best-kept secrets but my mom did find two love letters that I had written to a boy in my bag once, confessing my undying love for him. My mom was highly unimpressed by this dedication of love. My irritation was never that my mom had found the letters, though; it was that the letters never made it to the boy they were intended for.

Love letters would contain anything from song lyrics to poems and heartfelt messages. The aim was to have the prettiest and most colourful letter, and we really did try to outdo each other in this regard. Song lyrics were my favourite. I had a tiny multicoloured radio/cassette player, and I would pop in a cassette and press 'play', then listen to the lyrics carefully, then press 'pause', then write down the lyrics, then press 'play' again, listen carefully again, pause and write, and so it went until the song was fully written out, allowing me to sing it word for word.

If there was a boy that you liked, you would go to the public phones on the school premises. There was one that you could use a pay card on, which was a card preloaded with money. If the money on your card ran out, you could make a 'reverse phone call', which meant you could dial a specific landline number and ask to have the charges reversed. If the person on the other end agreed, they would then carry the cost. Many relationships and courting happened on those phones. There was one in particular that had a blurred glass door, and you could hear the giggles from inside that cubicle almost every afternoon.

Each year on Valentine's Day we would have a select few schools chosen that we could send roses between, and that was one of the highlights of the year. I was reminded not so long ago that I sent a hundred roses to the boy I dearly treasured – and still do, actually. I used my tuck-shop money to buy him the roses instead of buying food – I sacrificed my stomach to declare my love for him. He has grown to be an incredible guy who I speak to every now and again. I was speaking to him recently and he told me he is not surprised I am doing so well in my life and business; I always would have got what I wanted, he said, and I think he is correct. Once I am set on something, it is difficult for me to lose focus.

⁂

I always loved languages and the extra drama classes I attended, and of course I did the best in those subjects. When I moved schools for Grades 11 and 12, and found out that drama was an actual subject (not an extramural), my heart almost popped out of my chest in excitement: I could do what I loved and prove myself to everyone, and it would also contribute to my moving to the next grade!

Drama turned out to be a tough subject, but it was worth the effort and the intense exam preparation. Drama also helped me come out of my shell a little more authentically – well, that, coupled with my having what felt like a new start because of being in a new school without previous trauma having tainted my image.

That said, I never built friendships in that school quite like I did at the convent. My new friendships did not have the time to blossom quite like my convent school friendships – although, even those convent-school friendships did not blossom until much later on in life; but the seeds for them were planted while we were at school. These days, those women and I try to keep up with each other although our schedules are busy and we do not see each other as often as we'd like, but they hold a special place in my heart.

I always tried to fill my days at school with some sort of light relief. I would watch episodes of the American soap opera *Days of Our Lives* very carefully each afternoon, and the next day at school I would act out the scenes in a comical way. The character of Stefano DiMera, played by Joseph Mascolo, was my absolute favourite. And the character of nun Sister Mary Moira Banks, played by Eileen Davidson, had an overbite and spoke in a high-pitched voice, and I would mimic her – her scenes were crazy, and she would hurl insults, and complain and talk about Marlena Evans, played by Deidre Hall.

I was almost certain that I had found what I loved doing in essence – languages and drama, and bringing people together – and the other subjects felt like a waste of time to me. I had no idea how I would use these three aspects together in the future but they were my love and made my heart happy.

So, from an early age, I clearly could see the bigger picture in my love of languages, drama and bringing people together: they were the corner pieces of my life puzzle. And indeed, those things form an important part of the impact I make in the world today.

Remember that you are indeed an intricate masterpiece, and you have been from the time you were conceived. May you be encouraged to reflect on select areas of your life and begin to piece your puzzle together and define that.

You have to start with figuring out the bigger picture – even if it is blurry at first – in order to understand how each piece of your life fits together.

4

Embrace life's promises

Darkness cannot exist without light; both need to co-exist.

If you switch off the light in your bedroom, it immediately feels like you are in complete darkness, but after a while the light starts to settle in its own character. The light was always there but darkness has a way of portraying its inconstant power – if you look carefully, you always find light waiting for you to discover it.

Similarly, we must face life's challenges, and because these segments of challenges represent darkness, we sometimes give them unfounded strength. If we take time to reflect intently on our lives as individuals, we begin to see that life offers us glimmers and pockets of hope even within darkness. I like to call these clusters of hope 'life's promises' – the breeding ground for expectations of good things to come.

I have had many guardian angels in my life, people I believe were put in my path to help me, to hold my hand and to nurture me when I was falling apart; people outside of my mom who cared to direct and redirect my life without expecting anything in return. I have chosen to focus on one of these angels in this chapter.

But life does not only give us promises through people, it also provides assurance through events and situations. Can you believe one of my life's promises was through music and electricity? Yes, actual electricity that we use in our homes, cities and all around to light up darkness (when there isn't loadshedding!). I will use this specific example to show how most simple advantages for others could be the exact whisper from life for a promise to come.

When I was in Grade 10, my mom agreed to my changing schools – this was after my dad had once again moved out of our home. Moving to this new school meant that I could walk to school in the morning and back home in the afternoons because it was close to home. But the most fascinating thing for me about my new school was the fact that I was in a classroom with boys!

When I look back on this period, it was a moment of life's promise, and it reminds me that life's restart button is always readily available; we just need to use it.

I met one of my significant guardian angels at my new school in Grade 11. Sadly, she has since passed on, and my heart is broken because she would have loved to see my journey as it is progressing lately. She was my gorgeous English teacher, Ms Simpson. She was elderly and wise, and very good at seeing the unspoken and reading between the lines. She figured out quite quickly that I was just saying I wanted to be a computer programmer because I thought it was the cool thing to say to fit in, and she did not make it a secret that she thought that even insinuating anything to do with computers was a joke when it came to my future career.

When we spoke about career choices, as she often would with all the children, she would make it clear that she thought I was either going to be on world stages or be Madam Speaker in parliament. She made it clear that she thought I was born to be great and she could tell it was going to manifest. I would often be shocked by this because I could not understand why and how she saw so much in me.

She did not only predict my future, she invested in it, wholeheartedly. It did not matter what plans she had, if there was a speaking or debating competition, she would enter me in it, not only in English but in Afrikaans too. She knew that I had a single mom who sometimes could not take me to those competitions, and she would take me in her own car, her white Volkswagen Fox, if need be, without asking for anything in return. Her payback was watching me succeed at this 'speaking' thing. She also knew that I could not disagree to going because she had figured out that I had the world of respect for her: I never wanted to disappoint her, and I never did in this arena. The lowest mark I have ever brought back from a speaking competition was an A- and we both were super-upset about that A-! She made me feel valued, as though I was her ace card when it came to representing the school on these types of platforms.

When I reached matric, we had an external invigilator who would check a few of us to make sure the school's internal marking scale was in line and accordance with set standards. Usually, they would choose the top achievers in English, a few from the middle and a handful of the lower-performing children. We all had to have a prepared reading and a couple of other items.

I was one of the top students, with the highest English literacy mark, so Ms Simpson whispered for me to please prepare. I was also one of only two black children in my entire grade, and Ms Simpson was not shy to speak through how the world could perceive a black child getting the highest English mark; she thought alerting me about this perception would soften the blow if I got stares and under-breath comments from the invigilators. Unfortunately, back then, a black child speaking English the way I did was considered unusual. (In actual fact, I still get asked about my fluency in English as a grown adult!)

I was indeed chosen – and Ms Simpson need not have worried, as I was more than prepared. I wanted to help her shine, so I was determined to put my best foot forward. I aced the examination, and she was super-proud of my performance.

I loved Ms Simpson and she loved me. She dreamed for me, even if I did not believe her when she said that one day what she saw in me would all make sense. Well, what she saw in me is starting to sprout from the seeds she helped plant and is coming to fruition.

I took a long and winding road to get to where I am, but it would have never been a further consideration had it not been for Ms Simpson, my guardian angel, the one who believed in me when I did not believe in myself. I had come to the conclusion that making enough money to survive may just be the most important thing to focus on, and I was not sure my dreams would be able to sustain the bills, given the state of arts and culture in South Africa back in the early 2000s. My dream of being on world stages was safely tucked away in my bedroom with the roll-on deodorant (as my microphone), and that was it.

Ms Simpson was one of my most profound 'life's promises'. I am always grateful for her.

Let's cross the bridge now from human-led promises to circumstance-led promises.

The first entire music album I learned off by heart was Mariah Carey's *Music Box*. Now, there's an album that I still cannot listen to without flashbacks!

My parents gave me the album on cassette on my tenth birthday, together with my first and only Walkman, a small portable cassette player with earphones. I would pop on my earphones and listen to Mariah Carey's soothing voice all the way to Rosebank and all the way back – because of the long drive, I would listen to the entire album at least one a half times on any given day. Those were my private moments away from a world that could be noisy, cruel and unkind.

Oh man, I sang every lyric in my head, but I was too immature to understand their meaning. To this day, I love the song 'Hero'. Initially, I loved it for its melody, but in hindsight my subconscious was telling me each time I listened to it that I would be a hero: 'There's a hero / If you look inside your heart!'

It's a pity that I am not a brilliant singer, because if I could sing brilliantly, I would never stop. Yes, I can hold a note, actually many notes, but when I was blessed, I was blessed fully with a speaking and talking voice, not quite a singing one.

Mariah Carey really held my hand through her music, but when I was old enough and Mom taught me Céline Dion, I started to notice that the lyrics had meaning, that they allowed the expression of feelings in ways previously unimaginable. I always enjoyed riding in the car with Mommy because we would listen to Céline Dion's music on repeat: 'Baby, think twice, for the sake of our love, for the memories...' I know the entire album of *The Colour of My Love* off by heart.

It was a promise that something as innocuous as words could create an out-of-this-world future for me. I am now in a beautiful lifelong relationship with words – that simple promise was true!

―※―

I had to find ways to escape my day-to-day reality of never knowing whether the home I woke in would be peaceful or not, and music was one of them. Then, just as I began feeling that I was equipped to deal with my various issues, another painful reality arose.

Every year we had a school camp. These school trips were created to make sure that we children could take part in teambuilding activities with our peers, and they were also an opportunity for us to have hands-on learning.

We would pack our bags according to lists provided by the teachers. My mom is a perfectionist, and while she may think that she has failed at many roles and choices in her life, she was always the best mom according to her knowledge at the time, and she continues to be so in every way possible. She would double and triple check that I had everything on the lists provided, and would make sure I also had spoils galore when it came to the packed lunch for the bus ride. I do not remember finishing the packed lunch for any trip because there was always so much food!

I have become that mom now, only a notch higher – you best believe that when my boys have a trip, I am checking the lists and putting things together a month before they actually leave. The apple not only fell very close to the tree but grew into a larger tree!

On the morning of the trip, our parents would come to wave us off, and watch us as the bus drove away. My mom never missed a waving moment.

I went to one of these camps in Grade 8, and on our way back home, having been without TV and other home comforts for a week, I was excited for my Friday evening TV schedule: *Jam Alley*, then *Living Single*, then *Studio Mix*, with a few breaks in between. The bus arrived and my mom was there, diligently waiting for me.

I remember that I was wearing an outfit she so badly wanted me to have, and so throughout the week I made sure I wore other outfits so I could make her happy and wear that one for when I got back. It was a pair of jeans with a denim jacket and black velvet body suit (yep, velvet). I wore that outfit with pride to make my mom smile, because by that time I had realised that my mom's smiles were rare and shortlived – there were very few moments that was she able to fully be herself because she was always walking on eggshells around my father. She could not laugh too loud or respond however she wanted, as anything was a trigger for him.

I jumped into Mommy's car, and she gave me a hug. Then we drove a short distance before she told me that she had bad news. I automatically thought 'death' but it was not that. Still, she struggled to say the words, I still remember her face as she was talking; only as an adult did I realise how difficult it had been for her. 'We have no electricity at home,' she said.

I was sad because I had been looking forward to watching my TV programmes, but my initial reaction was calm because I thought it was only a temporary problem and would only last for a short period.

It was my father's responsibility to pay the electricity bills, and because he hadn't paid them for so long, what was owed was a high very amount. Our household was therefore considered a 'high risk' one, and our electricity was switched off until the account was settled. My mother, who always had savings, could have paid the huge bill herself, but she wanted my father to stand up and take responsibility – clever girl!

As it turned out, we had no electricity for just under a year. For almost a year, we lit our lives with candles and cooked with paraffin. I realise now that I had little to complain about, given that I have witnessed some children who live through that daily, and some who were in worse circumstances and situations than I was in – I can only understand that now that I have a larger concept of the world and its unfairness. In the bigger scheme of things, I still had food on my plate for all three meals, I still had quality education, I had clothes on my back and a roof over my head. Had you, however, tried to explain that to me as a young girl, I would not have gotten it.

If you have ever lived in a house with paraffin, you will know what damage it causes to walls and the smell it leaves on everything. This didn't actually bother me until a girl at school mentioned in front of everyone that my lunchbox smelt like paraffin. That led to my not wanting to eat my lunch or quietly sneaking items out to gobble them down without everyone seeing or smelling anything.

I tried to always plan to sleep at a friend's place on the weekends because this meant that I would at least have electricity for two days. A childhood friend's parents were gracious enough to always let me stay over with them at their welcoming home in Parktown North when I asked, because they had knowledge of the situation at home.

Living in a dark home for a long period of time was actually a blessing in disguise, as it gave me a lot of time to think and to imagine. My imagination saved me. I used my imagination to dream about my future. I would dream about how I would travel to gorgeous destinations all over the globe and work in those places.

Regardless of how bad things were, Mom always had a plan. We may not have had electricity but when a school trip to Mauritius came up, my mom came to the party.

When I initially took French as a subject, I only did so to be able to go on this trip, as it was an open secret that students who opted for French as an additional language would stand a chance of going. The school planned the trip every second year and, trust my luck, on the first year of the subject choice, it was the biennial due time to go. How about that! I did not even need to prove my marks; I automatically qualified.

When the letter finally came with all the details of the trip and the costs, my heart sank. The trip would cost fifteen thousand rand – a lot of money in the year 2000. Knowing that my father had finally settled the outstanding electricity account, and that it was almost the same amount as the trip itself, I felt my hope dwindle.

But I did not give up. I very sheepishly told Mom about it and the details of the cost. She immediately told me that no matter what, I was going. She would make a plan. She had savings, and she would use the money to pay for me to go to Mauritius, without a shadow of a doubt.

I almost did not believe her but she gave me her golden signature on the response slip with the 'yes' box ticked. She always made sure that I had the best opportunities, and if going international at fifteen meant parting with a large amount of money, then so be it.

Life's promise to you is sometimes loud and sometimes it whispers. And sometimes it just sits there, waiting for you to discover its existence. I encourage you to walk through life both consciously and intentionally. When you are aware, you are alert to the things happening within and around you. When you are intentional, you are deliberate about exploring the seen and the unseen.

The key point is to walk through life knowing that, no matter how discouraging things can get, life is always offering a promise in one way another.

> **Keep your promises to yourself, to ensure that life keeps its promises to you.**

5

When your inner voice speaks, listen

There are many things in life you can ignore, and in actual fact *should* ignore, because life is full of distractions. Life is full of people with opinions, and many of those opinions stem from people who themselves have not figured life out either.

I took considerable pressure off myself when I realised that I need not conform to any opinion by virtue of the fact that nobody has the rule book of life itself. Yep, believe it or not, we are all just winging it, every single one of us.

I do not listen too deeply to my emotions because my emotions are circumstantial and so they are not always factual. Emotions are always real, but they are not necessarily factual because they are based on feelings.

However, there are some things you cannot and should not ignore. These include the inner guide of our hearts and minds – our instincts.

Another two aspects I suggest you should pay attention to are, first, your mistakes; and, second, your health on all fronts – physical, mental and psychological. Mistakes never lie: when we make a mistake, we should learn a lesson from it, and try not to repeat it; and if we do make the same mistake again, we should at least try to take another, new lesson from the experience for growth to occur. And your health is a whispering friend whose warnings you can hear only if you want to; I suggest that you do listen!

I certainly have gone through periods of life when I did not listen to my guiding forces. I did not listen to my instincts, I did not look after my health, and I repeated my mistakes – and I paid the price. I went through these phases for longer than I should have by not listening. Take a walk with me down the aisle.

※

I am a chaser of love, love in every form. You will be guaranteed to find me with intentional friendships, relationships and people around me. It was without doubt that marriage was something I pursued until it forcefully liked me back. It did try to reject me, though, at first.

Everyone wants to be loved unconditionally and effortlessly by their significant other. We may not have the same dreams but the need for love is always the constant – even though it may be for different types of love.

Most young people (especially young girls) daydream of meeting their perfect partner and creating a life together. I was the same, and on top of that, I wanted to build the total opposite of what my parents had created. It was something I felt I owed to myself and my children. I wanted to show that I could have a happy home, and for me a happy home had to start with a happy marriage. I wanted to prove that love could love me.

I met a man I thought I loved at work (in fact, I met all three of my significant life partners in adulthood at work). Let's call him Owen. I had walked upstairs to a colleague's office and there he was, sitting working at her desk.

Okay, let's take a step back. Initially, I had called my colleague and she had put me on speakerphone. He was sitting there, and he heard my voice and was instantly attracted to it. He braved himself to speak over her and tell me that he was in her office, and I decided to courteously give him the privilege to match the face to the voice, and that's why I walked upstairs.

He was calm and shy; he was actually a nerd-like guy, with the glasses and all. I had been with enough 'roughneck' dudes previously that I knew he was a totally different personality to that, and I was intrigued by his nature and almost instantly charmed by him.

After a brief but comprehensive conversation, he asked me if I would give him my number. I said I would, but only if he actually used it. A few days later, he did, and we started to hang out quite often.

Owen was a ball of fun. He really was: he exposed me to so many new things, opened my eyes to so much. He was soft-spoken but had a touch of decent arrogance to him in the beginning. He was always laughing. He thought I was super-cool. I wanted to be super-cool to someone, to believe that this worth inside of me that I thought he could see was the potential I worked so hard to realise.

Why did I even care about what he thought of me, instead of being concerned about if he actually loved me genuinely? He had been exposed to so much more in life than me, and had travelled the world way more, and he had experienced the finer things in life, and that made me believe that I was in the right union. I had found someone who could help me reach far bigger dreams, and he would push me to achieve them.

When I look back at what I thought was exposure to these sophisticated things by Owen, I could almost roll on the floor with laughter compared to the exposure I have since experienced, but he did honestly help grow me up.

We dated for a number of years before we decided to get married. During those years it seemed like he masked my eyes to who he actually was. He comes from an extremely loving family but I never quite felt like I fitted in with them, for some odd reason.

I had the best fun planning our wedding. Whatever I wanted, I could get, partly because of how financially stable I was, partly because Owen was also contributing, and partly because my mom got way too excited – her only daughter was getting married, and it would be what her daughter wanted, at whatever expense, even if she had to pay for it! The wedding venue was Avianto in Muldersdrift. This venue has two chapels but I did not want another bride on the premises and that was arranged too – the entire venue was booked out for us (I mean, really?).

I am in all trueness a no-fuss girl, and anything that will require bells and whistles is not my cup of tea. This lavish wedding was to show off to others.

What I didn't know was that Owen borrowed money to make the portion of the planning allocated to him happen. I had no idea that he borrowed money from family, friends, colleagues (you name it) to finance aspects of our wedding. I only found this out two years into the marriage. There I was, thinking my life was bliss and I was living *la dolce vita* – until a small crack became a big earth-shattering gap.

Part of Owen's financial responsibility for our wedding was paying for the honeymoon. Two days after our lavish wedding, with over two hundred guests and all the embellishments, we were due to leave for France, which would be our first stop for a couple of days, before closing it off in Italy for the last couple of days. As I was packing for our honeymoon, I asked Owen how much he had put aside for shopping. I am big on budgeting, and I wanted to manage my own expectations.

In response, Owen told me that he had gotten himself into some financial mess and it would be a while before he could get himself out of it. Drawing my own conclusions, I assumed that meant a few weeks. I thought it was no big deal and did not make a fuss about it. I was on a high – I had just gotten married and my head was not in a clear state.

I had investments, so I told my new husband, no problem, I would simply calculate how much we needed and withdraw some funds for us to have a blast on our trip. We jumped into the car and off to the bank we went. It was a quick process to arrange the money – with heavy penalty fees for early withdrawals, though – and then went back home to finish off packing.

I thought I would fall in love with Paris immediately, like people always say, but I did not get that feeling. I warmed up to it in a few days in, though. (I definitely want to take a trip there again, to see if I get a different perspective.) Rome was okay, too, but my love was Pisa. I cannot pinpoint why but I loved that place so much and everything was just fantastic – the food, the ambience, the hidden treasures.

When we got home to South Africa, something was off. Owen had changed. It was almost as if he'd wanted us to stay in Europe forever – and perhaps he had, because it was a form of escapism for him. Because when he had told me he was in 'financial trouble', he had put it mildly, or maybe I had interpreted it in that manner. And now, back at home, the reality of life must have kicked in.

We had been living together prior to getting married. Actually, he had been living with me, and I had never questioned it because we were a couple. We had mastered the art of sharing bills and I was comfy with it but when this particular month end came and Owen had zero to give, things started to crumble. I really didn't care that much if he had money or not, because I was able to cover the costs, but, in all honesty, the spiral of empty promises and lies became my biggest issue during this period.

I should not have ignored the little hints of deceit – life has a way of showing you what to watch out for. If you listen carefully to most people, they will let you know who they really are through their actions and vocabulary. Do not try to paint a different picture when someone is trying to show you who they are through revealing their true colours.

Owen continued to imagine that he was living a life that he could never bring to reality, given the kind of trouble he was in. He would make up situations about how well his deals were coming along. He was a dreamer, but his lies became larger and larger, and his dishonesty became bigger and braver. He was continuously borrowing money from our friends without letting me know, and I was the idiot wife who had no idea until much later on that front too.

In fact, it turned out that our friends, his family and our acquaintances knew more detail about our household than I did. I hate this part because it means that every time I went to an event or a gathering, when I thought they were whispering about me, they actually were! Why did Owen put me through this when I could have made an alternative plan the way I always had? He robbed me of my dignity and the opportunity to keep our household matters our own.

He even drove me to a golf estate one Sunday. He knew I had always wanted to live on a golf estate (go figure!) and proceeded to show me around. What happened next was extremely embarrassing for me, but let me share it for people to learn and be cautious in future. He took me to the main office and asked them which stands were available. They showed us, and Owen convinced me to put a down payment on a piece of land on which we could build our dream home. He said he would then pay the balance.

My husband could not afford monthly bills, yet I still picked a piece of land and paid over a large sum of money on it, believing that he could turn this around for us. I was living in a soap opera, so unaware and yet so willing. I handed over my hard-earned money, and when the time came a few months later to pay the balance for the land, I got an email that made me spiral into anger. To that point, Owen had been getting all the emails, but he was ignoring them. A day before the due date for the balance, they finally decided to reach out to me, as they had not been able to reach him. The email was to communicate that if we were not able to pay the balance in the next 24 hours, we would lose our down payment.

This was so unfair! Had Owen told me in time, I would have made a plan to fix things, but he gave me no time to figure all of this out. I had no issues with him being in financial trouble at that point, but he strung me along and tied me deeply into his mess, and I was now suffering his inadequacy to husband fairly. Again, here, life was telling me that I so badly wanted to live the opposite of my parents' marriage that I was ignoring the hints that could have saved me so much hurt and pain. I do not regret going through those lessons because I was able to use them going forward.

But before things got better for me, they got worse for us. Owen started to abuse me verbally and emotionally. He would comment on my weight, and this eventually drove me to becoming bulimic. He would also comment on how I dressed. He was always worried about my wearing heels, as it would make me taller than him. One day my bestie, Khosi, came to pick me up for a party, and he would not let me leave the house until I changed – he could not have his wife dress the way she wanted and deemed fit as a grown adult!

It became a horrific household to live in – for both of us, as we both contributed to the heartache and chaos. I definitely played my role in the mess. It is seldom one-sided when it comes to matters of the heart.

Owen was verbally abusing me and cheating on me, and I was full-blown cheating on him and verbally abusing him too by this stage. One thing I can say in his defence is that not once did he threaten me or lift a finger against me or make me feel unsafe, and for that I am thankful. Still, I remember thinking that if this is what marriage was, with all this drama, I did not want it.

I finally realised that I was being pushed into becoming exactly what I did not want to become: I had wanted to prove that I could make marriage work, not be a part of a failing marriage. I decided to file for divorce, but it took me another year to actually proceed with it.

I was embarrassed that I had made everyone dress up to come to my wedding, and now I had failed at making it work. My personal assistant at the time, Lebo, could see how unhappy I was, and she was incredible (and still is). She held my hand and, when the time came, she went with me to the court, and she was the one who cried while I got the paperwork done. (I usually get things done and feel later; it is the nature of my personality.)

One of the toughest days of my life was when I had to ask him to move out of my house, and it's something I have never quite forgiven myself for. I asked him to pack his clothes in black plastic bags and leave; the only thing I was willing to offer him at that time were those black bags.

Owen made it difficult for the sheriff of the court to serve the divorce papers on him – he would duck and dive, and he prolonged the process. Eventually we got it done, but when contract-settling time came, he made it clear that he would make it difficult for me. The clause in question was the money I felt he owed me, and in that little brown office at the High Court, with no shame, he told me that he could 'play this game for another five years'. Eventually, I decided that the money was not worth it; my happiness was far more important, and I was stuck in my own life because of this clause.

Letting the money go was a big mistake because when tough times came I had nothing to fall back on. But here's the grace that comforts me: my son, Sakhile, who was around five years old at the time, now says he never knew that we were struggling financially (way to go, Mommy Thami), so I was able to shield him from all this painful drama and possible trauma.

The lesson of how resilient I am able to be was definitely one I will take on for life. But I also have to be aware that my resilience can shut me off from the world, and I carry a lot of weight on my shoulders. The problem is I am able to bottle up only so much until it all explodes, and the explosion is never pretty.

I was now out of what felt like a brutal marriage, but I was lost. The following few months would be all about trying to fill that void with several relationships that didn't last – and I did not want them to. In fact, after the divorce was final, I almost wanted to take Owen back! It was almost like I wanted him to come back so I could have a do-over, and handle things in a far more decent manner.

I am not sure if I can quite say if Owen was a nice person or not but he certainly taught me a lot about finances, about faux love and about the mistake of living life according to timelines.

Life is always dropping hints for us but we need to be still enough to listen, to be aware, because if we are, it will spare us so much difficult learning. Learning does not need to be painful if we learn the lesson quickly enough and the first time around.

Reflecting on my life, I realise that life had been teaching me the same lesson over and over again. I was too blind to learn it soon enough, however, and I therefore suffered until I was ready to accept the lesson. It was teaching me that I could not be happy with someone else if I was not happy with myself first. I needed to fix me, first and fully.

Life is your friend. As your friend, it wants to help you. Listen and observe the little things it shows you along the way. Do not ignore the clues life gives you, and use them to build the life of your desires.

Ignoring your inner voice may give you a theme you do not want in your life.

6

My two little lifesavers

If we were to live perfect lives, then we would be depriving ourselves of lessons and experience. Learning from mistakes means we want to do things differently next time, not that we want to erase the previous time we felt we could have done it better according to whatever standards.

I like many of my things in my life to be orderly but I am also learning that embracing and accepting certain things is fine. Sometimes all we have to do is look at our pieces on the floor, and embrace that they have fallen on the floor, and try to see what else we can build if the first build was an epic fail.

I had two significant moments in my life that gave me an opportunity to embrace and improvise, because staying stagnant was not an option. The births of my two children were moments where 'correcting' the past was not an option. I simply had to think on my feet about the way forward. My children deserved a fair chance at life.

Just before I had Sakhile, when I was in my early twenties, I felt like I had no real purpose in life. My career was going okay – I was working in the communications industry – but I had no sense that I was truly *needed*. I was continuing without weighing any risks. I felt I had no concrete purpose; I felt sort of empty.

One night I prayed, asking for a reason to live, and the reason came clearly and instantaneously, the one reason that would make me want to keep going. I had not considered having a baby before that but I felt that was the correct thing to pray for. So I proceeded to pray to fall pregnant – I was in a steady relationship with my then boyfriend, so it felt like the natural progression of life.

I asked God to please bless me with a child. I felt that if I had a child, I would have someone to work for, someone to love unconditionally and a reason to breathe. I was quite explicit and specific in my prayer; I wanted a little boy, a healthy boy who I could love and who would love me back.

The night I conceived Sakhile was also the night I asked for him. We were just ready to be in each other's lives. I think Sakhile was ready to come to earth, and he was ready to choose me, and I him.

Even before he was born, Sakhile and I fell in love. From the first time I heard his heartbeat – which was also the first time I ever had a sonar scan in my life – he gave me a bounce in my step and reason to keep at this life thing the right way.

I did not have much of my own materially at that stage: I had no car and no home of my own (I was still living with my mom) but what I did have was a baby that I had helped to create in my body, and I wanted him to have a beautiful, blessed and loving life.

My goal-driven way of living took over. I signed up for a medical aid, and I carefully bought all the things my baby would need. My son had the best of the best that I could afford – prams, baths, clothes, you name it. All his baby stuff was bought and in our home by month five of my pregnancy.

I also consciously started to save money – I'm big on saving for a rainy day. By month seven of my pregnancy, I had saved a couple of thousand rands – that was a lot of money back then, considering what I was earning and the sacrifices it took to save that kind of money.

When my belly was all the way out and I could not see my toes any longer, I realised that I really wanted a convenient life for this child, so I asked my mom if she could help me buy a car in her name, and I would work on getting my driver's licence. I had already made contact with the dealership, and I had enough money saved up to pay for the instalments while I was on maternity leave, and I showed my mom my bank statement as proof.

She was highly impressed. She agreed, and we proceeded to purchase the car. I trusted my cute black Kia Picanto, even though I later struggled to fit a pram in the boot!

I had already been driving for many years – the first time I moved a car without stalling was at the age of twelve – but because of the bad habits of driving I had accumulated along the way, I had failed the driver's test four times already. This time, I ensured that I got a driving school to help me with the parking techniques, so Bob would have to be your uncle.

With my learner's licence in hand and my mom by my side, I drove to the testing venue in my own car. The baby in my belly, kicking and all excited and very present, made it tough to manoeuvre the steering wheel. An hour later I had passed – fifth time lucky!

And so my life fell into place, not only for myself but for this baby boy I had asked for. Sakhile was born by emergency Caesarean section. I had wanted to try for a natural birth but my boy chose another way to enter this world.

Just before Sakhile turned a year old, I traded in my Kia for a silver Honda Jazz in my own name, and moved into a two-bedroom apartment my mom had bought as an investment; I rented it from her. She could see that I wanted to be fully independent and that I was ready for it. Any extra money I got went towards my new home, to buy a fridge, utensils, cutlery, a microwave, you name it. It felt like I was breathing for the first time in my life. I was in control and I knew I wanted to have a bright future – bright because I have potential, not because it would be filled with flowers and petals.

That is how my first son came into my life and saved me. He gave me the title of 'Mom' but he has very well lived out the meaning of his name ('builder of nations') thus far and will continue to. My Sakhile has continued to build me and be the foundation of the strong woman I aspire to be. I am certain that he will be a builder of others in whatever he chooses to become. He is a bringer of joy, loathing injustice and loving peace, a quiet human who carefully monitors and studies his surroundings, who picks up details in situations that fly right over my head at times. He is the yang to my yin, as our personalities are very different.

I will forever be thankful for this boy's life, and he will always be my baby. (Thank you for choosing me when I needed you most, my baby!)

When Tony (my second husband, but my favourite husband for life!) and I started dating, having another child was not an 'if, but or maybe' conversation; it was a guaranteed agreement, both vocally and non-verbally. We were standing in the kitchen one day, and I took the pills out of my handbag and flashed the pills at him and asked if I should stop taking them. He said 'yes' without hesitation, so into the dustbin they went.

Most women who want to have a baby do not think it will be them who struggle to fall pregnant – something so sacred and so blessed should honestly be a guaranteed gift to all females who desire to have a bundle of joy. We had prayed for this baby. We prayed hard, we prayed heavily, we begged God for this one.

But nine years is a long time to be on a medication that alters your hormones and regulates your body. Because women who use birth control pills for five or more years are more likely to have thinner endometrial linings, and a thin lining can make it difficult for an embryo to implant and result in a pregnancy, it took me a while to conceive. It was about eight months before I started to feel my body changing. The mind is such a beautiful thing – it remembers things that you thought you had long packed and stored away – and I had flashbacks of how my body had felt in the early days of my pregnancy with Sakhile.

Initially I did not want to say anything to Tony but it was tough because I tell this dude practically everything. He was away travelling, and I took the test at home and it came out positive. I did the natural thing and called him to let him know. We were beyond excited but I wanted to remain calm because I had read how tough pregnancies can become the older you get, and I was now in my mid-thirties.

The day before Mother's Day we opted to tell the family that we were having an addition – but our excitement was shortlived. Two weeks after confirming the pregnancy, I was struggling with stomach cramps. Then the worst thing happened: I started to bleed. The drive to the hospital was terrible, with both of us grieving separately. Seeing that sonar machine and hearing no heartbeat when you are expecting to hear one is an indescribably awful feeling.

A few hours later we were faced with telling everyone the painful news.

It was tough, it was hard, it felt like my heart had been ripped out from inside me. I felt as though my body had failed me. It had known how to carry a baby before, so how come it was confused about what to do this time around? I tried to trace back what I had done wrong: had I eaten the wrong food? Had I pushed myself too hard? The questions were endless, and not being able to find a concrete answer made it even more difficult to process.

The next day the boys really tried to make Mother's Day special. But on that day each year since then, there is always a moment when I take time to acknowledge what happened. It is not that sad for me any more, but you must take your own time healing if this has ever happened to you. There is absolutely no set time frame for healing.

But it was not long before I started to feel strange pregnancy symptoms again. Initially I thought it was just the after-effects of the miscarriage. But your gut knows; your gut always knows.

This time around, Tony and I were together when I did the home test, and it was positive again. Tony was happy but worried: he wanted everything to go seamlessly this time around. Fortunately, that is what happened: I had a fairly effortless pregnancy with my Sedi, although I did gain 30 kg from start to finish! This was partly because I was so worried about miscarrying again, so I refused to exercise or skip a meal even when I was not hungry. I was happy to sacrifice my health for this baby to come out healthy and happy.

When I went into labour a few weeks earlier than my due date, I had no idea; I just thought I was having uncomfortable pains. Still, Tony drove me to the hospital, and we were told that the baby was on the way.

Sedi's birth was a lot easier than Sakhile's, as I knew what was going on and the C-section was not an emergency one this time around. But for that reason I was also far more emotional; I knew that they were cutting through many layers of my body, and I had read enough to have a fear about what could go wrong. But everything went smoothly, and Sedi was born, another beautiful healthy bouncing baby boy. Sedi, my second son, is my big ray of light to this world; and that is actually the meaning of his name.

When it comes to the way you bring your baby into the world, I have friends who have had natural births and some who have gone the operation route. I say do what feels right and is the safest for you and your baby.

Sedi was a sweet baby, and he is still a sweet – and very vocal – boy. When he is not happy, he knows exactly how to express his feelings, and obviously he does it in the most age-appropriate manner. This meant, before he had the vocabulary to express his feelings, we sometimes went through periods of screaming fits. Thank goodness that phase is over!

Still, I now understand why we had to let the screaming and expression of emotions happen that way. I believe that if we try to tell boys how to express their feelings when they are young – or, rather, how to suppress their feelings – we cannot expect them to know how to miraculously express their feelings healthily when they are older. It does not work that way. Let your children express their feelings in an age-appropriate way, as long as they are not harming anyone, and they are not acquiring and building bad habits such as rudeness and disruptive disobedience.

In truth, my last-born son is in every way my personality. I always try to imagine how this is going to work when he is older – we will have to create a schedule for speaking and listening to each other effectively; we will have to set rules on how to engage and effectively communicate with each other.

Sedi really is the light we needed, and he shines so super-bright. He is a firm believer in fairness, even at an early age; he does not like to see anyone sad, and if someone is crying or hurting, he will offer a hug to make it better. He knows love, and he will continue to share love with the world.

He teaches me about patience, about kindness and about taking risks. This boy has no boundaries when it comes to trying new things, and is equally determined when he decides he does not want to do something! We tried to get him to ride a bicycle and he just refused. He is, however, more than happy to hop onto a pony!

Both my babies are answered prayers, and I will continue to thank God for them.

> Love is written in permanent ink, so you cannot erase anything.

7

Who are you?

A simple question that is super-difficult to answer for most individuals is, 'Who are you?'

At one stage, when I was in my early thirties and struggling with what direction I should take in life, I saw a career coach who had come highly recommended. In one of our sessions, she asked me to name the top five people I trust. I rattled off three names, and she asked why I had not named myself. Had I ever disappointed myself, she asked?

Indeed, I had disappointed myself before; on some occasions I have indeed let myself down. But it has never been to a point where I could not recover. No matter how bad things have become, I have still managed to get back on track to continue pursuing and creating.

But from that day forward, I grew to trust myself, to trust the vibes I feel, my thought processes, my decisions and my preferences. I could only do that once I had grasped who I really fully was – the worst of the bad parts of me, my best of the good, and the unattractive ugliness.

I believe that who you are should be an indication of the central part of you, the part that directs everything else about you; the part that does not change, regardless of the circumstances.

Had I been asked 'Who are you?' in my childhood, I probably would have answered by giving my name – and although your name is a form of identification, the truth is that my full name has changed three times in my life, so it cannot be my central core that holds me together.

In my twenties if you had asked me who I was, I would probably have given an answer that was fuelled by my abuse, or by my fighting against abuse.

I had met Vernon, the boyfriend I had at the time, through work, and we'd dated for about eighteen months. We'd broken up because I felt he was stifling me – he was very instructive, and I feared I would never reach my full potential with him as a partner. (He was the first, but by no means the last, in a long line of father replacements.)

I had a new car and I could easily get around, which meant I could drive to the movies and to friends just to get some fresh air. Vernon tried to reach me one evening when I was watching a movie with an acquaintance. I decided not to answer my phone, and he kept on calling, and I kept on not answering because we were no longer together.

So he decided it was a bright idea to drive to Mom's home, where I was living, and sit in his car with his lights off in a road close by and wait for me to arrive. Well, that is what I think he did, because a few minutes after I got home, he called me, and it was just too coincidental to be a coincidence. This time, I picked up the phone. He said to come to the gate (which was locked, as usual) because he needed to speak to me. I knew he had a temper on him but I was not afraid of him in any way. I am so glad that I agreed to go to the gate because I was openly shown a side of him he had hidden so well.

He asked where I had been and I did not answer the question; it was not his right to know my every move. Because I refused to answer, he reached through the gate to try and grab me. I managed to jump back in time. I could see that he quickly came to his senses after he pulled his arm back but he had shown me enough to determine what he was capable of, and so my love switch turned off, never to be turned on again when it came to having feelings for him.

How do you apologise to someone you almost harmed? With flowers, of course! He bought me a bunch of flowers and had them delivered to my office. They were the ugliest and smelliest flowers I had ever received. Not once did I water them. I wanted them to die as soon as possible, to rid me of the burden and reminder of what had happened.

(I could have just thrown them away but that solution did not come to mind at that time.)

From that day on, flowers and I have never gotten along. How dare someone think that giving a bunch of flowers will fix everything? I also feel like flowers are such a quick fix and a last-minute attempt at covering up when you have forgotten to get a meaningful gift. So now I dislike getting flowers as a token of appreciation or having flowers in my home – plants, yes please, but flowers? Keep them very far away from me. If you want to make feel unappreciated, and as though there was no thought process in choosing a gift for me, get me flowers!

That was the first time I chose myself and my son over an abusive relationship. The second time was in 2016, when I was 31 years old, and I almost took my life because I was defining who I was based on my circumstances and not on who I was at the core.

I had just started a new job, working as a senior account director for an agency. I was living in my own place, and had just bought a speedy machine of a car, which meant I was able to comfortably explore the world. I seemed to have all the material things that society paints as the requisites for true happiness. I felt like finally my life was on the up and up.

My boyfriend at the time, Ian, and I got to planning a vacation to Rwanda, partly because everyone who's been there speaks so profoundly and honestly about this unique gem. We were going to spend a few days in Kigali, Rwanda, and then travel to Mombasa in Kenya, where a friend of my partner had a house right on the beach, and from there we were going to go to their private game lodge, a five-hour drive out of the city, where we had a guaranteed viewing of the big five.

It was such a beautiful planning and preparing process for a few weeks that I could not stop talking about it to whoever cared to listen. I had hardly travelled in Africa (outside of South Africa) at that stage in my life – I had been to Nigeria, Nairobi in Kenya, and Swaziland, and that was it. So this was a big deal.

What happened the day before the awaited trip should have been an absolute indication that something was off. The signs are always there but we may choose to ignore them. It was without doubt or good reasoning that I chose to ignore the signs and to compromise my soul instead, and when I reflect on this, I am saddened that I chose an experience over my better judgement, all in the name of memories and temporary excitement.

That day, I was the programme director and host for an empowering event for women in the meetings, incentives, conferences and exhibitions industry – ironically, all while I was about to give away my own power unconsciously, like a piece of unconsidered zilch.

Ian, who lived in Cape Town while I lived in Johannesburg – so it was a kind of long-distance relationship – had been quite difficult to reach. I had phoned him many times but he had not picked up. We had made an arrangement that I would fetch him from the airport, and we would sleep over at my place, and then set off on our holiday the next day.

So I finished off my duties at the event with a smile on my face although there was turmoil happening inside of me. I was a tad concerned about how he hadn't been in touch, but I wrote that off as nothing to bother myself about. We were going to explore Africa together the next day, so surely nothing else should have mattered?

But as Ian walked towards the car at the airport, where I was waiting in the 'drop off and collect' zone, I could see that his face was red. I knew what that meant but I did not want to believe it. Then he got into the car and I could no longer deny it. The smell was too strong. He was completely drunk.

Now, I have no issues with people enjoying alcohol, but those who consistently abuse alcohol to the point of being drunk raise the hairs on the back of my neck and send me into a spiral that I have worked hard to untangle myself from for the past few decades – it actually scares me. It's the kind of trigger that makes my tone and facial expression change in a split second, that trigger that sends a message down your spine that danger is lurking and trouble is brewing.

So there I was, almost twenty years on from the little ten-year-old girl struggling to find peace and meaning in a home terrorised by an abusive alcoholic, and almost two years into this relationship, in my car at the airport, admitting that I was with my dad again. The only difference was that this guy had blond hair and gorgeous blue eyes.

To be fair, Ian and my short relationship had not been plain sailing, and drama between us was nothing unusual. Because of the long-distance nature of the relationship, it had taken many phone calls and many flights to make it work. There was a lot of back forth to each other – which Ian always planned. He would always get mad if I considered dropping in as a surprise.

At that stage, he had never physically abused me, and I believed that he did not have the ability to. Like any couple, we would argue, and I would always be the one to apologise. He was brilliant at spinning the story so that I was the one in wrong in every situation – what we now call 'gaslighting'. He was good at that, and when he 'explained' the situation, it was always clear that I was indeed 'in the wrong'. He was good at driving and controlling my emotions. He had isolated me from most of my friends and family, and so I had him mostly to rely on. As far as he was concerned, he was my 'Clyde' but I was not his 'Bonnie', because only he could be the main character in this story.

Many people close to both of us had not encouraged our dating and relationship. Only a few had actually been happy about it, and I think that was partially just the fascination of this interracial couple overtly going through drama; it was like we were a living in a soap opera.

Well, I did not care what people thought. I loved him and I was going to make it work, regardless. Notice how I said 'I' there, not 'we'? He had had many partners prior to me, and those relationships had never worked out, but I, Thami, was going to fix him!

Just before my first trip to visit him in Cape Town soon after we had started going steady, he had actually just come out of a rehab – I mean, really, Thami? But I did not care about that. Humans all make mistakes, so I never feel the need to judge because, trust me, I have my own fair share of matters I can be rightfully judged about. So I was determined to help this man get better and heal. I thought I had finally found my happiness, and he dangled that happiness in front of me like a carrot I could never quite grab because he always held it just out of reach.

I had allowed the abuse monster to follow me from childhood all the way into my adulthood. I had watched my dad be abusive, and my subconscious brain had agreed that that was what love was supposed to be. As long as I was not being beaten up like my mother, it surely was not abuse; it was just 'lovers' quarrels'. And when they were over, it was always me who would grovel in apology. Please understand that when I say 'grovel', I am not using the word lightly: I would actually grovel for him to forgive me and love me, as in my eyes I was not worthy of his love.

I was stupid not to see the signs. Actually, I *did* see the signs – but perhaps I so desperately wanted to be loved that I ignored them.

Anyway, so on that day at the airport, Ian jumped into the car and he hardly said anything to me. I asked why he had not answered my million calls that day (it felt like a million, okay?) and why he had decided to drink. He knew about my past history with my alcoholic father, and how triggering excessive drinking was for me.

He simply demanded that I drive. In actual fact, he threatened that if I make a big deal about him being drunk, he would no longer go on the trip with me and he could not care less. He knew very well what the trip meant to me. Never mind that I had paid my own way for the holiday, I felt oddly like I owed him for taking me along to introduce me to his friends, so I had to obey his rules like I was not a grown woman with a say in how I wanted my life to run.

So I drove us home without any arguments, and fortunately nothing particularly eventful happened that evening. I was only too happy to keep it peaceful so that I would not upset him any further.

We got up quite early the next day to make our way to a different airport to embark on our long-awaited Rwanda holiday. I was excited. I love travelling and an adventure. I am intrigued by the tourism industry, how vast both leisure and business tourism are, how they boost the economy. The tourism industry has become a treasure box I enjoy opening each and every time.

When we landed in Rwanda, it was love at first sight for me. Rwanda had this feeling of peace, safety and wonder. You felt so welcome there, and you knew that you could simply be yourself and you would not be judged nor harmed intentionally; there were army representatives on the streets ready to fearlessly protect everyone. I loved the greenery, the scenery, even the friendliness of the gentleman who was taking us to our hotel.

Our hotel was beautiful, with an amazing rooftop view, so we dropped off our bags quite quickly and went up for... yes, you guessed it – a drink. That one drink became many but that was okay because we were on holiday and we were relaxed and so why not? We were also very happy together that day. He took pride in showing me around and he even tried to convince me to move to Rwanda permanently with him, because he believed we would have a better future there.

That evening, however, to my huge shock and horror, I got a message on Facebook Messenger to warn me that Ian was not only living with another woman temporarily, but also sleeping with a third one. The message came from a woman I'll call Sylvia. She was the wife of one of Ian's friends, and she knew what he was up to behind my back. She could no longer bear to watch me being lied to and betrayed, but she did not have my number, so she had searched for me on Facebook and left me a direct message there.

So, while I had thought I was building a life with this man, another reality was taking place. How was this even possible? I used to travel to Cape Town to visit him quite often, and he visited me all the time in Gauteng, so how had he managed to pull this off? (I later learned that every time I visited him at his home in Cape Town, he would have the house cleaned up and not leave a trace of the other woman's belongings, not even a hair band or pin, to ensure that I had no idea what was going on. I later found out that he had a bad drug problem, and that he also brought prostitutes into that home that I considered 'ours' when I visited him in Cape Town.)

I asked him if the message I'd received was true. With tears in his blue eyes, he admitted it was. And I could tell that he was not sad because he had no remorse about his despicable behaviour, and because he had been caught out.

He went back to our hotel room, but I decided to stay on the rooftop and continued to drink. Weirdly, instead of being upset with him, I was upset with Sylvia – it was a case of shooting the messenger. Why would she feel the need to meddle in my business? It did not concern her!

One thing led to another in my mind, and for a few seconds I considered jumping off that roof. I was tired of love not loving me, and I was tired of feeling like I did not matter. This had gone on for too long with the men in my life, from childhood right up until that point.

However, I thought of my precious young son, Sakhile, back at home with my mom, and pushed that suicidal feeling away. I reminded myself that I did have people who loved me and needed me.

The next few days of our vacation were filled with the most lavish apology gestures from Ian. I kid you not, he must have said 'I'm sorry' at least twenty times each day. He wanted everything to go back to the way it had been as quickly as possible. But this was not because he loved me. Rather, his dating me was all about the fact that he had found himself a 'put together' girl, and if he could show up with me to the world, it meant that he too was put together – or so he thought in his mind. I was his robot, and I had no permission to feel and process for too long, because if I was honest about my emotions, that meant he would no longer be able to keep up the pretence that he was perfect and living a perfect life with his girlfriend.

Ian proceeded to propose to me only three days after I had found out what secrets he had been keeping. He asked me to marry him, spontaneously, on a mountain top in the middle of Kenya. He went down on one knee, and promised me the unattainable moon and stars, and also an engagement ring to follow.

My desperation to be loved and to feel valued led the way, and I answered before my brain could catch up – I said yes.

That very night, he physically abused me for the first time. Drunk, he tried to bite my finger. After the fight that followed, he opted to leave our shared room and go and sleep elsewhere. But I was afraid he would come back and hurt me, so I crept under the bed and slept there.

So the night of my proposal, in a country I was unfamiliar with, in a lodge that had roaming cheetahs outside, I spent sleeping, in fear, under a bed.

That was a turning point for me – feeling like I wanted to jump off that rooftop in Rwanda, and then being physically abused by someone I thought I loved and who I thought loved me, had brought me to my senses. I knew I needed to talk to someone, and I found the courage to explain to some loved ones what was going on. They helped me to begin to piece myself back together, so Ian did not have as much of a grip on me as before.

Ian did not let go easily, and a few weeks after the trip, he phoned and begged me to fly to him in Cape Town. Before Rwanda, I would have dropped everything and gone to him, but my heart had started to become hard towards him and I refused. Sadly, he passed away not long afterwards, as a result of his lifestyle.

Although by then I had moved on with my life, I always felt horrible that I was not able to 'fix' him and help him face and come to terms with his childhood traumas; I felt as though I had failed him.

Despite the horrible things that had happened to me there, the trip to Rwanda was beautiful in the sense that it was there that I realised that the pieces of my soul were lying shattered on the ground, and that I began to pick them up and rebuild myself. My circumstances had fooled me into defining who I was according to them, and I was no longer going to allow that to be the case in my life. After long consideration, I finally decided I am not a girl who deserves abuse; I simply could not define myself that way any longer. I had the choice of whether I wanted to allow abuse to be a part of me or not going forward.

With much silence and consideration, and many tears, I decided I finally defined who I was. I was learning that it is not about choosing yourself in a haphazard manner; you have to choose yourself wholeheartedly each and every damned time. I had taken the journey of asking who I was and starting to dig deep within myself to find the parts of me that have stood strong since childhood, and which continue to stand strong, regardless of situations and circumstances.

I hope that my sharing how I was able to define who I really am, even after my circumstances had wanted to define me as something else, will open your eyes to your circumstances and remind you that situations change, and that who you are cannot be defined by them. I am hoping the insights I discovered will show that you, too, can sit quietly and search deeply for the true meaning of your existence.

I hope that sharing this part of my story with you will provide you with bravery to look beyond your crisis, your sadness, your tender circumstances, and to push through and dig deep and discover who you are. Once you know who you are, nothing will hold you back. The foundation of your discovery will stand the test of time because your foundation is always built to help you stand, and rarely does it crumble.

So, stop and ask yourself, 'Who am I?' If you cannot define it yet, do not despair. But I do challenge you to continue asking yourself this question until you begin to identify the good parts of yourself and to discover which parts hold you up each time life tries to break you down. If you have not uncovered it yet, it is there, waiting to be uncovered. It wants to play its part and be considered.

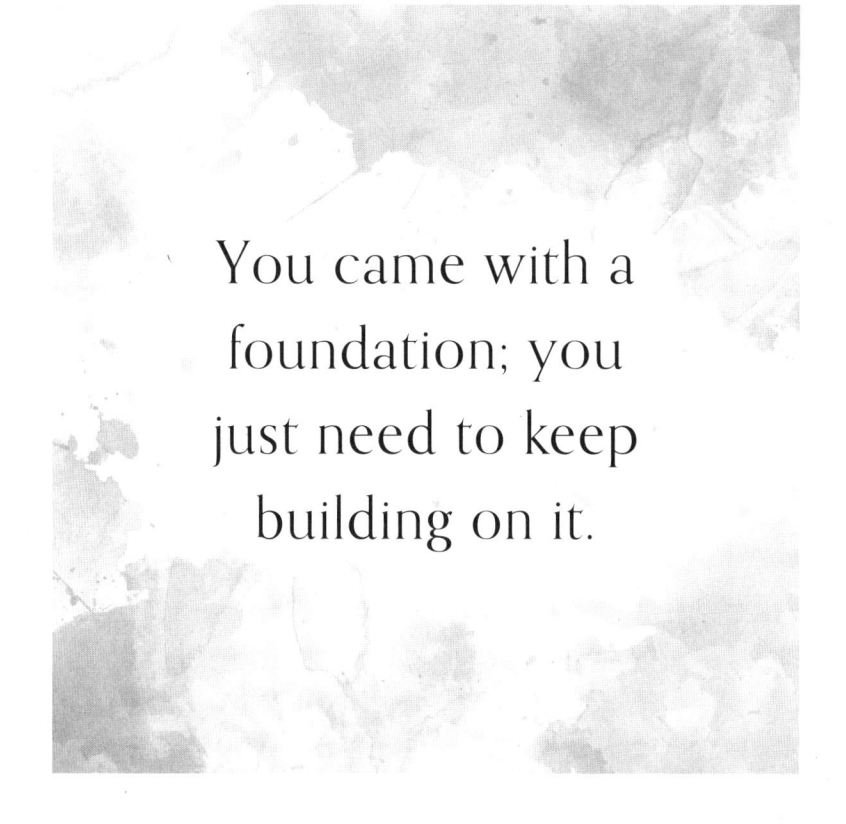

> You came with a foundation; you just need to keep building on it.

8

Be truthful to yourself

I have to come to understand that you cannot be truthful to others without being truthful to yourself. You also cannot fully move in the direction required without completely being honest with yourself.

These words fall super-simply from the lips but they are not easy to implement. Truthfulness requires vulnerability, but because we are taught to protect ourselves from a young age, it is not natural to fully expose ourselves for the sake of growth and fulfilment.

Nothing is ever actually buried when it comes to our life experiences. If you think it is buried, you are just avoiding it, and that is not true vulnerability.

When I decided that I was going to fully commit to being Thami Nkadimeng the public figure, I realised that I was opening myself up to the world for compliments but also for judgement. Sadly, that was indeed the case. If you want to make any form of impact, you need to expose yourself to other humans, and humans come filled with opinions, and those opinions are sometimes not positive nor dressed fairly or appropriately when dished out.

I have had to find a way to be comfortable with some of the things that are not so cute about my life, and I have had to fully unpack them, because if I have unpacked them, there is absolutely nothing uncomfortable about them being discussed by others on my behalf. If others speak about my past, for example, I have the power to provide details to the story, as I was there, making those mistakes myself, but I can only fully do that if I am comfortable with opening my own closet to reveal the skeletons.

There's one particular area in my life I had to be honest about, and it was a very touchy one.

I have had bouts of introspection over the past few years, wondering why I have sometimes had such 'bad luck', as I would call it, and I would like to share my thought process on two aspects that I believe are often confused. (This is, of course, from my own perspective. Perhaps it is not confusing to you, but as I engage with other humans, I have heard it come up in conversation.)

Success may be defined differently in different families and individuals, but when I reflect on my family history,

I was always afraid that success may not happen for me because of the minimal track record of success in my family. I was also not sure whether I would be successful partly because of how success was described to me, and defined as material gains, and modelled as a shortlived experience. I have since realised that success has a much deeper meaning for me.

I am an African, and in our culture, we tend to believe that success is most often blocked by elements outside of ourselves; often, we explore the idea of being cursed if we believe ourselves prevented from achieving success. It is not easy to blame ourselves, so instead we blame these curses, and so the vicious cycle is perpetuated, with nothing fixed and with no clear and permanent direction forward.

I am well aware that these types of evil may exist, because everything under the sun becomes a reality if you believe it does. But for me and my loved ones, I have declared and continue to do so, that if there are curses, those curses will not affect me and mine in any way.

Some people feel they are the victim of 'generational curses', which are curses such as unhappy marriages leading into divorce, or not being able to hold down a stable career, when in fact the issue is past trauma that is repeating itself. I have certainly made this mistake, for how do we even start to unpack generational trauma when our native language does not even have a word for it? How do we even start the conversation when the very outbursts of trauma may be defined as one going crazy?

I know families, including my own, in which the trauma of three or more generations prior is still affecting the current generation. It is a difficult cycle to stop but it can be done. It takes conscious and intentional living, and you have to remain consistent and persistent and determined to break it.

First, you have to acknowledge the trauma actually exists. We all have past family trauma, and it needs to be truthfully identified. In my case, it was the horror of living as a child in a family beset by alcoholism. Until we acknowledge these traumas, and our responses to them, we are doomed to repeat what we know or what we have seen.

This is the vulnerability I am talking about: the honesty of admitting that a problem was present in your bloodline and that it could have affected you in some way. It requires immersing yourself in the history of your family, because to build you must know what else existed on the land you're building on. It's not a simple thing to do, but when done right, everything else will stand properly.

If, as in my case, you had an abusive father, and that was the only love you knew as a child from a male figure, it is easy to fall into the trap of repeating your response to that trauma, even if this is often done unconsciously. I think it goes without saying that most parents do not intentionally wish their children to struggle with the same circumstances as they had to face in their childhood. But this behaviour repetition can be a vicious cycle, happening over several generations.

In my own case, as I have mentioned in previous chapters, I started to pick up a pattern in the type of men I was choosing for myself: men with 'disciplinarian' traits, like my own father had. I was also attracted to abusive men, and some who were even alcoholics themselves. Almost always, these men had not grown up with a father, and/or had had to man up too early because they believed they had to fill this gap and become 'the man of the house'. Perhaps they had been referred to as the man of the house by the adults in their lives, and that subconsciously gave their brain a message that they were in charge – but to a youngster with raging hormones, and especially those in societies in which toxic masculinity is a problem, 'in charge' can often manifest as aggression.

I chose to bring an end to this generational cycle for the sake of my children. I did this by praying for a husband who had all the opposite traits to toxic masculinity. This meant a conscious choice of being aware of those negative traits and wanting to be to be attracted to the opposite of them.

Your trauma may be the same as mine, or it may be different. Either way, we need to equip ourselves to deal with our trauma so that we can help create healthy societies. I chose to start this rebuilding with my own household, as it is a space that I am able to guide and take full ownership for, in my own way and with my own methods. You may choose another starting point for your own rebuilding, such as what you do not want in life and making a conscious decision to attract the opposite of it.

One important thing we have to be cognisant of when dealing with past trauma is self-sabotage. Self-sabotage is a subtle monster that does not shout or make a noise. Rather, it nudges you bit by bit to make decisions that are not beneficial for you. This could mean that when opportunities come your way, because you have not unpacked your past baggage or admitted to it, you will unconsciously push away the glimmer of light wanting to shine. Self-sabotage comes with behaviours that can prevent you from reaching your goals and dreams.

Not being able to ask for help is a form of self-sabotage. Asking for help is good, and it is even better when you ask for help from people who can actually help you! My self-sabotaging came in by my wanting to do everything by and for myself, because we were taught that you must not share your plans because people would curse you – but how are you to achieve your goals without help, honestly? The trick here is to share with the correct people at the correct time for the correct reason.

I now have no shame in asking for help and opportunities, because how else will the opportunities be presented to me? Through my ceiling, miraculously? Everyone needs help sometimes – yes, even the CEO or MD you are admiring or the celebrity you look up to (believe it or not) has asked for help from someone at some stage, and that someone has opened a door or two for them.

If you do not work on your behaviour of self-sabotaging, you will train your brain that these are the correct ways of life, and they will become who you are, and difficult to undo at some stage. Identify them sooner rather than later, and let's stop mixing up potential curses and past traumas.

Another 'demon' we have to look out for is impostor syndrome. This is when you have the feeling that you are not good enough, that you are not worthy – because how dare you win? But I ask, how dare you *not* win, after all the effort you have put in to your dreams and goals, and after the battle you are continuing to wage by simply waking up every day to face whatever comes your way?

Personally, in order to get over my own impostor syndrome, I had to learn the difference between seeking genuine advice and needing approval. When you start something of significance from scratch, of course you want to be praised for it – but there is a distinct difference between genuine praise and a crippling need for approval. I suffered from not knowing the difference for a long time in the foundational phase of my career, and it still creeps in now and again. I am thankful that my life keeps me so busy now that by the time the approval comes, I am usually on to the next thing!

There is a flip side to this, where getting publicly applauded and commended can sometimes leave me superembarrassed. Of course, I do want to be acknowledged for my work without feeling shy about it. It is a matter of balance that I am working on. I try to process my wins firstly with myself, then with my family and friends, so that by the time I share them with the world, there is no longer any need for the approval. I will get it right one day.

One of my early struggles involved constantly comparing myself to others, and finding myself wanting. This came about partly because I am by nature a perfectionist. If I could not do something perfectly, then I was not going to do it at all; but while I was not doing it, I was watching someone else do it, and seeing their way as perfect – and this ended up making me feel 'less than'. I got over this by learning that I was good enough and that no benchmark is suitable because we are all our own benchmarks.

Next, I had to let go of any form of potential addiction – and this means addiction not only to substances, but also to behaviours and attitudes. It is easy to want to show the world how successful you are, and that can become an addiction itself. In this regard, the addiction can be to what label you are wearing, what fancy restaurant you're eating in, the size of your home and the make of your car.

I understand where this stems from, given that many people are the first in their homes to achieve these kinds of success. But if you look carefully at those consistently showing off these kinds of lifestyles – usually on social media – you may discover that there is some sort of trauma or lack in their past, and that they are still deep in that trauma, and now feel the need to forcefully show the world how they have made it. They want their subconscious to know how much they have come through, and they want to share it with the world as a form of personal validation.

For me, I made a conscious decision that in my success I would have boundaries; I made a pact with myself and those close to me about what I would and would not share about my personal life – I had to learn the difference between transparency and openness.

Trauma seems to happen to people more and more lately, and it may seem like a fantasy to try to escape it. But the sooner you admit your traumas and work on them, the better, because nobody else will work on them for you. One way to put this is to stop bleeding on people who did not cause you the wound, as they say. Rather, work on yourself in every and any way possible, to be the best version of you.

And when you do work on your traumas, do so in truth. Knowing honestly what we come from can be completely overwhelming but it is not something that is unworkable. Being truthful to ourselves may be painful at times but it does enable us to live authentic lives.

Being truthful to yourself does not mean not listening to the opinions of others. It means being able to look into your life and, no matter where you are, admit that no matter what has happened to you or in your family in the past, you have the opportunity to forgive yourself and those who have done wrong to you.

Being true to yourself is not just about blurting out what is on your mind. It is about living by your beliefs, and at the same time giving yourself permission to change those beliefs at times, when you know better.

Living your truth should not feel exhausting. Rather, it is about being able to be human with consistency, whether in front of others or alone in a dark room late at night.

It is not about wanting to live for praise; rather, it is about living with acceptance being an option, not the driver of your life.

Being truthful is about acknowledging parts of you that may not be acceptable socially, and sharing them anyway, because you acknowledge that you are a work in progress.

Being truthful is being able to look at the things you really need and want, versus the things you feel you need to have to be well regarded.

Being honest with yourself is understanding yourself completely, because you know yourself best.

Everyone has skeletons in their closet. Take yours out and give them a decent burial!

9

What's love got to do with it?

Just in case you have not gathered, I am an African girl, and a South African-born girl specifically. I know you have journeyed with me this far but I like to remind myself of my heritage every now and then, because I can. And because I am proud of it. I am a lovely mix of many tribes, with a touch of westernisation here and there, too. But my core is African at its best.

For most African children, church is a non-negotiable when you are young and living in your parents' house. Well, it was this way when I was growing up. Tradition and routine dictated that on Sundays we would put on our best clothes and off to church we went. For a young girl like me, 'Sunday best' comprised of a pretty colourful dress never short of frills, white patent-leather shoes with a buckle, worn with frilly patterned knee-high socks, and pigtails tied with ribbons.

I used to be fascinated by the church congregation as a young girl, and how they sang the songs. Each adult would come with a Bible and a song book, but the way they sang the songs was as if the lyrics were being dragged out. They knew when to stand up and sit down, in sync, and it felt like a lot of standing and sitting.

Whether you remembered what was preached about or not three minutes after the service was neither here nor there, as long as you had ticked off the box to get to heaven every Sunday. At least, it felt like a box-ticking exercise to me.

Once church was done, we would head home and watch the adults cooking a multicoloured meal, including ruby-red beetroot, yellow savoury rice, bright green spinach, and so on. This traditional 'seven colours' meal was so named because it was supposed to contain all the colours of the rainbow.

(The box-ticking exercise of going to church on Sunday may have been exactly what I needed to direct my life, and I still go to church on Sundays. However, I do not conform to the seven-colours lunch tradition. You see, I quickly figured out that the preparation of this large and often elaborate meal was the responsibility of the woman in the house, and while I enjoy cooking, I cook when I want to, not when it must happen on schedule. So I stay very far away from promising a tradition that I cannot uphold.)

After lunch, most kids went out into the streets to play with other neighbourhood children, although I was often not allowed to do so because my parents thought the streets were 'too dangerous' for me – truly, I lived the most juxtaposed childhood! (Sometimes, I would be allowed to go out with my bicycle and ride a little bit under the careful supervision of Manie, my nanny.)

The home I lived in with my mother and father from birth until I was nine years old was in Protea North in Soweto. It had high walls with brown gates, and an intercom at the gate so that we could talk to anyone who arrived before deciding whether to let them in or not. It also had electric garage doors. So it had very tight security – but it was the one place I felt the most insecure and unsafe.

Instead of being allowed out to play with the other children in the street, I would be locked up in the yard with my dog. My first dog was a Maltese poodle called Fluffy. I loved him dearly. I did not even consider him a dog; rather, he was my baby, and I would carry him around in a blanket like a baby and even dress him up – I knew about creating dog fashion before it was a thing! If I was going to look good, then so should Fluffy.

One day Fluffy went missing. He never left our back yard, so this was a mystery. We searched and searched and searched but could not find him. Then, hours later, he just turned up at the gate – I think dogs are so smart, and my boy found his way home! I was so excited to have him back.

He seemed fine and quietly went to sleep. He never woke up again. We have always had a suspicion that he was poisoned.

That was my first experience with death, and I carried its scars with me into adulthood. I had not just lost a puppy, I had lost a family member, and a friend I hung out with on weekends, and the one who always knew how I felt – I had lost my best friend.

My children have been asking for a puppy over the past few years and I am keen to give it a try but I will have to let this feeling of sudden loss go before I can fully commit. Luckily, I have my husband Tony to shield me, as he does not want a dog at all – he did not grow up in an environment where dogs were allowed in the house. I think he is secretly afraid of falling in love with the dog and having to admit that he was wrong about pets!

After Fluffy died we got another dog. We named him Sieza. He was very different to Fluffy – he was a big Alsatian – but he quickly stole my heart. He became my partner in everything naughty, but he also offered protection to our yard. He helped me out when nobody else could at that young tender age – for example, he would eat my lunch for me when I had not finished it at school, and this allowed me to confidently tell my mom that my lunchbox was empty when she asked.

When we moved to our new house in Randburg, my parents decided to donate Sieza to the Protea North police station. I was not ever told why we could not take him with us, and I was never given the chance to say goodbye to him, as they came and took him while I was at school, and again I was ripped apart.

We had several other dogs after Sieza but I never quite connected with them because I was too afraid to – I didn't want to get my heart broken again.

When we moved to Randburg, we also had to change churches. While walking in Cresta Mall one day, a lady with red hair approached my parents and invited them to attend her church, and they were excited to try it out.

The church turned out to be fantastic. It had different sectors, such as one for kids, one for teenagers, one for singles, and so on, and all these ministries had fun activities and different events to attend. I was obsessed with the singing ('worship', as it is fondly known), which was my favourite part and still is.

It was very family oriented, and we all built long-lasting friendships there. The cool people I met there and made friends with were raised with similar principles and in similar environments to mine. I get super-excited when I see these individuals because they have known me for decades. We have an unwritten code of love between us.

Church was great in that it taught me about God, friendships and making the correct choices. I honestly believe that if I was not in that particular church, I would have long been a mess.

With every silver lining there is also a cloud, however. Some of the people I met at that church can be counted among those who have hurt me the most; they would make me comfortable enough to share my innermost feelings and desires, only to turn around and gossip about me behind my back. They would lure me in to talk about the kind of man I want to be with, for example, and figure out who my crush was, and then go to that person and tell him that I was not a 'good influence' for him.

While church was a really great place to be, I have come to realise that we put certain individuals on an unfair pedestal to lead us at times when they themselves are just humans. My first proper encounter with leadership was in church, and I was indirectly taught about hierarchy and titles there. Over a period of time, I gained enough courage to realise that God never was or is the problem. The problem is people I expected too much from. Had I figured this out earlier, it could have saved me so much pain and misery.

I watched how leadership works and how people in leadership can make or break others, especially those who could be considered to be much lower down in the metaphorical food chain. As individuals, we may think the lessons we gain from mentors, coaches and bosses is what to do, but some of the best lessons are what *not* to do, which we can learn through their actions and mistakes.

Through this period, it became clear to me that mentoring could also be a narrow way of thinking, if it meant you were only mentored by one or two people. What about the lessons you are meant to learn from everyone else you meet and engage with as you journey along in life? Surely you cannot base your lessons only on the people you are familiar with, when there is so much opportunity to learn from all individuals who have a story to live and tell on this earth?

I have chosen to make the entire human race my mentors in whichever path or career they are in. This part of my healing journey allows me to 'see' everyone because I know how it feels to not be 'seen'. This does not mean that I am fully present and tuned in to all lessons when I am around people all the time – if I tried to do that, I would go mad. Rather, it means that when I catch a gem from someone, I store it in my knowledge bank, regardless of who it came from.

Some of the coolest and smartest people I have met in my life have been the ones who are often not considered so. I make a conscious effort to converse with the security guards, the cleaners, the cashiers and the petrol attendants of this world, because more often than not, I get a gem, if not many, from them in any given conversation.

My whole journey in church has taught me to know my place, and to speak in turn when allowed into someone's life. It has taught me to know that there is a time and place for everything. It has taught me to know the difference between having an impact and bulldozing.

People go to church because it is a place of refuge and comfort from the issues they have, whether it be health, work, finances, personal battles or relationships. Church is the place where most people feel connected to their Creator. It is important that people feel secure and welcomed in these places, because we have no idea what they are going through once they leave that congregation.

I am almost certain that church will always represent love for me, and that love need not be perfect. Because of how love has sometimes been interpreted to me in the past, I believe I was always loved but it was not interpreted in the most acceptable way. I am almost certain that people would not blame me if I did not believe in love any more. I am filled with gratitude that despite the hardships I have gone through, I have not allowed them to take away or to destroy my heart and the love I want to spread to the world.

Love comes in many forms – family love, childlike love, career love, failed relationship love, parental love, self-love and so on – and I ask myself if I know the definition and feeling of love in its true and pure form. I believe that the reason I had to go through the first thirty years of my life was to understand how to define love in a way that makes sense to me for the remainder of my years – and I know there are going to be many long, beautiful years ahead. It was all gorgeously orchestrated so that I was able to appreciate what I have by having experienced some of what I did not want as part of my life. How else do you define the option to choose if you have not experienced the alternatives?

To me, love is a choice. It is loving myself and others enough, when 'enough' is relative and a target for you to set yourself. It is knowing that we evolve, and that for that evolution to fully occur, we must have room to change our choices. I can guarantee that the choices around love that I made a decade ago are mostly not the same decisions I would make now. I am thankful I made decisions the way I did back then, but I have developed over the years, and I am still developing.

Love to me is embracing. It is embracing those to whom you want to give affection but also embracing the ride of life. It is taking the time to take it all in and to reflect on what a journey it has been and is still going to be, given the privilege to live.

Love is such a unique experience. Nobody has had or is having an identical love experience to anyone else's. Even the partner you love is having a unique experience of love.

For me, love is knowing that a higher power thought me worthy to be created and to be protected by Him, even if I make an epic mess of it all. He is right there to dust me off when I cannot dust myself off, and to give me a pat on the back to encourage me to keep going, to give it another shot.

Love is sacrifice – not sacrificing yourself but sometimes sacrificing certain perks and pleasures to be able to make someone else feel worthy, seen and appreciated.

Love is being so secure in who I am that I do not need to bottle up my emotions. It is being able to settle misunderstandings in a caring and affirming manner. It is sometimes giving up the chance of being right to rather allow the chance to communicate openly for the next person. Being right can come at a heavy price.

I encourage you reflect on your life and to see how love has always popped up but perhaps not always dressed in familiar clothes. Did you notice love? Did you learn from it? Did you give it room to grow? Did you mould it or did you allow it to mould you – because how can we even start to preach kindness if we have not understood the very basics of love?

I asked a handful of my friends to explain how they think I have developed in loving, and how I love now, as an example of how you can check in to see if what you feel inside is aligned to what you're giving back to the world, or if you're autopiloting from past hurt. (I am a 'words of affirmation' individual too, so this exercise served a dual purpose!)

Khosi Nkosi, who has been my best friend since I was five years old, and who I consider my sister, said,

> Love is patient. Love is kind. For me, this definitely describes my friend Thami. I have been through so much, and Thami's love is consistent, comforting and everlasting. She is a lover and a giver, and she is of course an outspoken one, so she will give you a piece of her mind while supporting you. Even in trying times, she is able to bring light, love and joy. I'm honoured to be within the inner circle and to be blessed with such an amazing and wonderful friend.

Another best friend, and someone I consider my 'human diary', Lerato Moloantwa, said,

> Thami is not shy to tell you how much you mean to her. She is happy to hear from you every time you reach out. She genuinely gets excited when you share your good news with her. She enjoys being part of your human journey. She always gives compliments and asks about how you are really doing. She praises the hard work that you do. She has courage to remind you how grateful she is that she knows you. She always encourages you to reach for your dreams. She does not shy away from telling you what she has learned from you. She always makes time to share a moment.

And my only male bestie, Lefentse Makoko, said,

> I hope this encourages you to never let hurt change how you love, how you receive love and, most importantly, how you give love, because without love we are lost.

To experience the full spectrum of love is to experience both the magic and the pain that it holds. That way, you will love wholeheartedly and fearlessly through the peaks and troughs of your life in an uncompromising way.

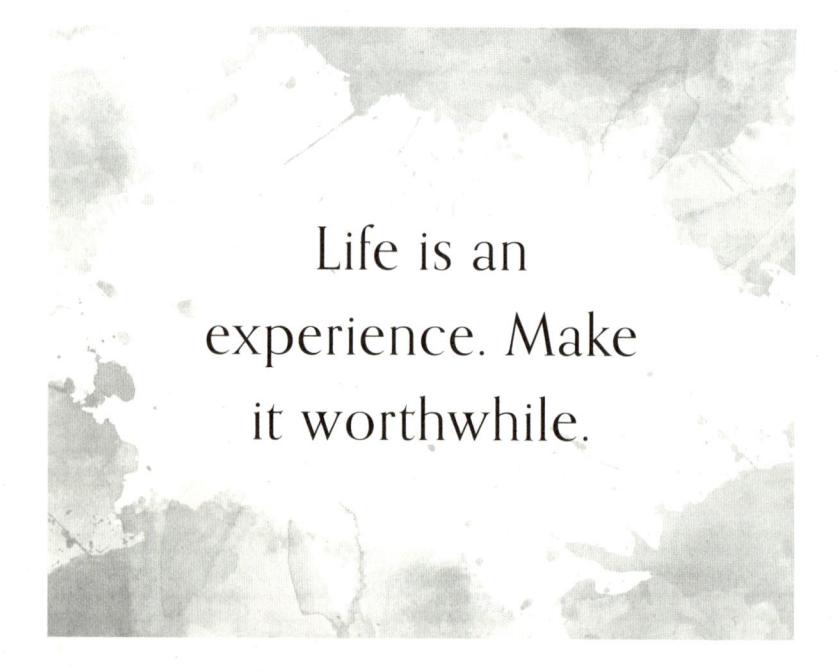

> # Life is an experience. Make it worthwhile.

10

Crossing boundaries in life's journey

Boundaries define an area or areas that cannot be accessed without permission, or areas that are controlled by rules and restrictions that have to be adhered to in that particular space.

We see in life that boundaries exist everywhere. Life has become so dangerous and risky, requiring protection and guarding, that we do really require boundaries. We have boundaries to where we can travel without permission, we have multiple boundaries for our homes, and we have boundaries around our personal spaces.

For borders to hold any sort of weight or recognition, there must be mutual agreement between the creator of the border and the person wanting to cross that border. Without this, the importance of the border is non-existent.

We are all individuals, and we each have boundaries to what we can achieve and what we cannot achieve, and this is why we all have different talents and skills. The contradiction here, however, is that these boundaries are a myth. These kinds of boundaries are a form of self-limiting beliefs: we give credit to them because we will then have an excuse for why we could not achieve more than we should have. We give these boundaries credence, limiting how far we can grow or how much we can achieve, because then if we do not reach our full potential, we have something to blame other than ourselves.

The truth is that nobody's life journey has any boundaries. We all have full capability to achieve whatever we want to achieve. There is no passport to success; there is no visa to growth. It is a free-for-all in this division, and the ones who are willing to explore far and wide are the ones who will reap the satisfaction of the unrestricted possibilities to be achieved.

At a certain time of year, there is much chatter and talk around the matric results, and when this happens, I cannot help but reflect on my own matric year. This was my second and final year in a new school. I had settled down to some extent but I was also struggling to adjust in some respects. I was a teenager trying to juggle the many changes happening at home – my father had finally and officially moved out – and I had not adjusted to our new rhythm. Mix this with hormones and you have a beautiful pot of confusion.

When we wrote our preliminary exams for matric, I failed all my subjects except English and Drama. I do not like to fail but I had so much I was working through in my mind and heart that I was spiralling. What made it worse was that I had thought I was prepared for the exams. I had put some time into studying but in honesty I did not really put in the effort – I thought I would just cruise through the exams. I was completely wrong.

My mother and I were called in to the office of the school because the teachers were afraid that I would not make it through matric finals. In South Africa, preliminary exams are an indication of what the student knows, and it is believed that how a student does in these is a reflection of how they will perform in their final exams. However, it can also be an indication of how badly a student wants to pass the finals, because failing prelims can give you a massive scare. This is what happened in my case.

I had just over a month to get my act together. Failing matric would have shattered me – I had never failed or repeated a grade in my schooling career, and I was not prepared to start now. Fear took over. I imagined what it would feel like to not see my name in the newspaper when the national matric results were published – back when I matriculated, in 2002, your surname and initials were printed in the newspaper for the world to see on the day of results release. I was going to make sure that my name would be there.

I studied for those final exams like my life depended on them – honestly, because I felt it did. Matric results were your gateway to further studies and then to the world. I was focused and I was not going to cause my mom the embarrassment in full view of an audience who may have been watching (known and unknown) – funnily enough, this has become the story of my life now, being in the public view.

The date when the results would be printed was announced on the national news, and the night before, I felt like I was going to lose my mind. I couldn't eat, and I went to my bedroom an epic mess to try and get some sort of shuteye – I figured that if I slept, the morning would come quicker. I had no such luck; I just tossed and turned the entire time.

Around five thirty the next morning, I got up and went to the garage across the road to buy the newspaper, but they were already sold out. I refused to go home without knowing my results.

I walked to school and waited there. I knew that at least one teacher would have the official printed copies of our results.

After what felt like a lifetime, a teacher did arrive, and she was shocked to see that I had not even showered (although at least I had brushed my teeth!). Seeing how stressed I was, she quickly put my heart at rest, telling me we had a 100% pass rate, meaning that all the school's matric students had passed.

I felt a huge weight lift off my shoulders. At that stage, I did not care what my marks were. The most important thing was that I passed.

So I made it through matric, with university entrance. I had proven to myself that I was capable of absolutely anything I wanted to achieve. That was a moment that indicated to me that my journey in life had no boundaries, and that any boundaries I thought were there only existed in my mind.

The manner in which I got my first job was perhaps an indication that my working life was going to be a ball of fun and an unpredictable bowl of ingredients that would eventually come together to make something delicious – skills and passion finished off with a drizzle of talent and a large dollop of purpose.

'Purpose' is a concept I had to understand and which I often speak on. To me, purpose is the intersection where passion and talent meet. The two are both vital to purpose; there are, for example, some people who are talented but who lack passion. Nelson Mandela, for instance, was a talented boxer in his early years but that was definitely not his passion, and therefore it was not his purpose.

In my case, I am extremely talented at putting events together, from conceptualisation to implementation and execution, but I have absolutely no passion for the attention to detail it requires. Thank goodness I have now landed on the other side of events, where I am part of the event. My past experience of putting events together has, however, made me very understanding of the organisers, because I understand what it takes to put a successful event together.

An example on the other side of this equation is the 'wooden microphone' category in the talent-search competition *Idols South Africa*, for people who have a passion for singing but not necessarily the talent for it!

This reminds me of when I was young and dreaming of being behind a microphone. I initially thought that my imagination was telling me to be a singer – that singing was my passion – so I asked my mom to drop me off at the auditions for *Popstars (South Africa)* one morning. I did not even make it through the preliminary round but it was a great experience – I found out that while I may have loved singing, I did not have a talent for it. Today, I use my microphone to help others have constructive conversations and to be the golden thread in conversations, ensuring there is direction to achieve objectives at any level in a hierarchy. It is both my talent and my passion – it is my purpose.

Life has a beautiful way of bringing together the passion and talent for you in an attempt to give you tools to reach your purpose – I have never met a person who is living out their purpose and who does not have both the passion and talent for it. I encourage an exercise to undertake if you are struggling to figure out what your purpose is. It will require a bit of time and complete honesty, and you will have to try to be objective. It may not give you the answer like a loud-sounding gong but it will certainly give you an indication and direction towards the correct route.

Write down all your passions. Next, write down your talents. Now review both lists and try to determine which passions and talents can co-exist. You could be passionate about healing people and talented at understanding different personalities, for example, and this could lead you down a medical route.

My career certainly did not start with my passions or my purpose. Shortly after I'd finished school, I accompanied my mom to her work year-end function one Saturday night, and while we were there, one of the executives asked what I was busy with at that point in my career. I explained that I had just completed my matric final exams, so technically I was now unemployed.

He said he was fascinated by my personality, and he offered me an entry-level job on the spot. I started working the following Tuesday. My salary was fairly high for a seventeen-year-old girl, and where I could pay to help our household, I did. It was often with buying groceries to offer some relief to my mom, and to feel important and necessary too.

At the time, my mother was driving my grandfather's old car, and I liked the idea of her getting a car for herself. This was partly why I decided to maintain my financial independence by continuing to earn money by working, and not to go to university, where I had applied to study IT.

I didn't consult my mother and about my decision, and she was super-mad at me. She wanted me to get quality education and further my studies to open up doors of opportunity. At the time, I was too busy dealing with my trauma to understand her feelings; I was not even coping with my own.

I went on to work odd jobs here and then – in call centres, selling vacuum cleaners, that kind of thing. I didn't earn nearly enough to run a household but it paid enough to have spending money while living under my mother's roof.

Finally, when I was nineteen years old, I landed a job at a firm of chartered accountants as a personal assistant. This exposed me to a completely new world – that of numbers. For a period of time the numbers world chased me: I was offered a role at another accountancy firm, where they agreed to let me do my articles over five years instead of three, so that I could do a BCom Accounting degree.

But the truth was that numbers were neither my passion nor my talent. I wanted to talk! Although I had an image of myself holding a microphone and being asked to go on camera in various areas and surroundings that were sometimes not safe, I knew that journalism was not for me; I have simply never found it appealing.

I discovered corporate communications just by being inquisitive. I wanted to speak for a living, and I thought corporate communications would be an entry into talking for a salary. So I began exploring degree options that would allow me the option to steer narratives. It made sense that I would pick communications as my choice of further studies because I thought getting a degree in this subject would mean I could use my verbal and non-verbal voice to impact the world and make a difference in society.

Although corporate communication over the years has proved to be less talking and more research than anything else – researching media, researching surroundings, researching tonalities, researching environments and societies, and so on – I am overwhelmed with gratitude that I discovered this gem. I have since obtained three degrees in communication and marketing, through distance studying, all while working and being a mom too – overachiever much?

When it comes to my career, I eventually landed in the economic development space in communications and events. This gave me an opportunity to dive into events, marketing and communications, science, innovation and technology, and tourism. I have come to believe that all the sectors I worked in are now playing a significant role in my moderating, because for years I was so intertwined in the subject matter of these various industries. Moderating conversations about these sectors feels like my paying them back for all the education and knowledge they have given me over the years.

I have also worked in the mining and construction sectors, and this really matured and moulded me. To have a senior portfolio that was a beautiful mix of looking after communities, managing the media, batting for my fellow executive committee team and being the voice of the employees was the best rollercoaster I have been on in my corporate career.

At some points – and I must be frank and raw on this one – I just worked to put food on the table and to provide where I needed to. I worked so that I could live to face another day, and that is okay, too, because even in those moments there were lessons on how I needed to trust my abilities, no matter the situation or circumstance.

I think it's safe to say that I took a roundabout way to achieve the impact I wanted, and to land up where I am, in moderating, programme directing, and human engagement through architecting messages. I choose this space wholeheartedly, regardless of the good, bad and ugly it comes with. This is because it is more than just a service I provide; it is where my heart is filled and where I fill, where I water and get watered, where I help others flourish and where I am nourished.

Nobody has to have it all figured out in their late teenage years or early twenties. What I focused on was obtaining comprehension of the various sectors, of the world, of humans and of the direction I wanted to take, and building on that. No learning is ever a waste of time.

In life, you are given the task of making some puzzle pieces fit together to get the clue to the next pit stop. I am still nowhere near a destination, and I know that my career trek continues. The comfort at this stage in my life is that I now, figuratively speaking, have boots to wear and a pair of binoculars for checking out the surrounding terrain; and I have other tools, too, that help me navigate my way to the top of the countless summits I still need to tackle.

Given my experience, my take on life's boundaries is that if boundaries in life were an actual thing, I would not have been allowed by life to exchange and move so freely through so many areas, dabbling and trying out different things, before I was fully convinced of where I wanted to stay and grow. If boundaries were a thing, we would all be born with one chance to make things work out the first time around. If boundaries were a thing, we would be given passports instead of birth certificates when we landed in the world.

If you believe your goals are being blocked by borders, figure out how to get a lifetime visa!

11

I'm a bestselling book in life's library and so are you

One day, in the shower, I asked God, why I am uniquely made? I know there must have been a reason that He had taken time to carve me out and breathe life into me, but I had not yet figured out why. Then a little voice in my heart said, you have not used your voice, and your voice is the essence to your answer.

I was confused by this because it sounded all a bit too complicated for my brain to break down and understand. But sometimes turning points present themselves when we feel we have faced the most tragic moments and have hit rock bottom, and the only direction is really to try and find a way up because there is nowhere else to go.

As with most things in my life, my turning point came right on time. Everything in our lives knows well before we do that it belongs in our lives at that very point. It is for this reason I believe that our lives are long planned before we arrive here, and also why I believe that we have to have been intentionally made.

My turning point wasn't so much a point as a process – it happened bit by bit. This made me realise that turning points can also be turning processes, and take effect over a period of time.

Three years ago, I had no idea what my purpose was or how to find it. I knew that at that point I was on a hamster wheel and chasing something that was not meant for me. I was chasing the wrong thing – my heart, brain and gut were not in partnership – and so I was struggling to feel fulfilled. Most of my days were filled with work that I was no longer passionate about.

As I began my career, I dreamt of becoming a CEO one day. To me, that meant being the chief executive officer of a large existing business – a massive one, a stock-exchange-listed corporate that was known for having highly skilled people at the top. To try to achieve this, I worked myself to the bone in every sense – long nights, strategy after strategy, deliverable after deliverable – all in the name of climbing the corporate ladder.

I gave it a good run and I got pretty close, but that type of CEO position was never really meant for me. The more I watched corporate CEOs, the more I saw how internally miserable and lonely it could get in those roles. Sure, I wanted to be a CEO – but I wanted it on my own terms.

So I tried another angle. I wanted to be involved in a corporate, but I wanted to dance at a different rhythm and pace, so I carefully put together a proposal to pitch to an executive at the company for which I was working at the time, to suggest that I become a consultant. I was brilliant at my job and I thought it was a no-brainer that I would be given the opportunity to break the shackles but still be able to use and offer my skills and knowledge.

They did not go for it. I intended to resign from my position as a communications executive at the end of March 2020. But then, just days before the month's end, President Cyril Ramaphosa announced that South Africa would join other parts of the world in a national lockdown that would last (initially) one month.

I spoke to the relevant executive, expressing my concern about jumping ship at that stage. The executive was happy to let me stay on: they had wanted me to stay anyway, as I was of value to the business. In hindsight, I am so glad that I did not jump ship then, because over the next two years, I would gain knowledge and insights that were valuable to me as an individual and that would help me in the long term.

I started to watch and listen to individuals talking and sharing opinions on social media. During that period, as people saw less of each other physically, and digital communication became paramount, everywhere we turned we would see Instagram, Facebook and other social media platforms broadcasting or streaming interviews and conversations.

I used the time to keep quiet and observe. In this, I had to do the total opposite of what my journey would require of me: I had to remain silent. In order to finally find my voice, first I had to keep quiet. It was surprisingly both easy and difficult to do. I wanted to have opinions and contribute, but I didn't want to simply add to the noise. I had to be the audience at that stage. It was an opportunity to exercise my listening muscle – because my contribution to the world would certainly require that listening muscle to be in tip-top shape.

What I started to notice was that these conversations were not always about pulling together for the benefit of humankind. They were often conducted by people speaking out of fear, speculating, sometimes even pessimistically.

It was through this process that I realised I am a builder – an architect. I build with my wisdom, my voice and my experience. I architect messages and conversations that impact humanity positively, whether it be through corporate contributions to humanity or on subjects that affect us all globally as people, humans and society.

It is beautiful how everything happens for a reason, absolutely everything! Had I become a consultant for that company, I probably would have not found my purpose at the time I did. Having my proposal to become a consultant rejected by that executive was not a failure after all. It was me being redirected to my true course of life. It was an opportunity being offered to me by life, and for that I am thankful.

That's how I eventually became The Message Architect. The title was not created out of pure cleverness but rather it was bestowed on me in a spiritual and supernatural sense. It was placed in my gut without doubt, and unless this has ever happened to you, it is a difficult feeling to explain. It was a whisper from the heavens above that only I could hear.

At the beginning of 2020, I was very certain of my purpose: I was starting to find my adult voice and finding out how to use it too. My childhood voice had been all bottled up inside, and so I felt that I had found a new instrument, and as is the case with any instrument, I needed to learn to use it properly for it to have melodic notes that would interest others and create 'music' that could be listened to. If you do not learn how to use an instrument effectively, it may still produce sounds but they could be considered distasteful.

Once I had figured out how to use my voice, although I still had to refine it, I knew that I wanted to use it for matters that impact the human race in a positive way. I'm a fighter in my heart, and even though I no longer feel I have to battle as I had to during my growing-up years, that fighter is still there, inside, and I doubt she will ever go away. I needed to channel that energy in me to benefit others and to make an impact.

The 17 United Nations Sustainable Development Goals seemed to me to be a space in which I could serve. These goals represent an urgent call for action by all countries to end poverty, improve health and education, reduce inequality, spur economic growth, tackle climate change, and preserve our oceans and forests, and they need all hands on deck.

I wanted to take the road less travelled to my mountain summit, so I knew I would have to start immediately. I embarked on this journey with no idea of what the summit looked like and no idea of what I was actually climbing but fully aware that it was all going to take effort. That is the thing about purpose: once you find yours, you feel as though you cannot waste any further time on things that do not matter, and you must pour your everything into achieving goals along the way related to your purpose, and it can feel that it needs to happen as fast as possible.

If it had been up to me alone, you would have seen me holding hands with some individuals who care about global societal changes in the first year of moderating conversations, and we would already be fighting together. But although my conviction was 100% there, I had to realise that to play in a band, you have to rehearse, and you must observe too.

I've learned over the years that if you build without a plan, things can come crashing down. The foundations and direction of it all must be well stabilised and supported. It is better to approach your purpose and impact with consistency. Doing things too quickly may make you feel as though you are riding high but you may have left gaps in your rush to rise.

So I made a tough decision: I chose to let things fall into place as they were meant to, in their own time, and with their own impact and direction. The time will always come for things to work out that should, and I am not running against any clock. Things happen when they are meant to happen and if they are meant to happen.

For all these reasons, I chose the route of consistency rather than intensity. (I am, however, starting to accelerate the intensity now too.) This journey taught me that all that is meant to will come to you if you welcome it and receive it with a pure heart and intentions.

This taught me that indeed some pieces have to fall apart in order for them to all fall back into place. While the world was in chaos and uncertainty, I was the calmest and most in tune with myself and the world that I had ever been in my life.

Although I was still formally employed full-time, the seed of The Message Architect had been planted and it had continued growing, slowly and quietly. It was an extremely busy time. I continued to build my business brick by brick, while I had a demanding full-time job. I worked very long hours – I could not let any of these balls drop, and I was still little Miss Perfectionist! It was exhausting but the fire in my belly kept me going. I used to remind myself that nothing worth it is ever easy, and I knew that juggling both these roles while being a mom, wife, daughter, friend, you name it, would pay off eventually.

When I wanted to go and moderate conversations for my various clients in the different provinces of South Africa (this was before I became a global name), I had to take leave from my full-time job. This was not too much of a problem when I was starting out, but as The Message Architect lit up and more and more people were asking me to moderate, my leave days could not keep up.

Something had to give.

In 2022, the day after that disastrous rehearsal for my TEDx talk, I was called in to a meeting at my office. What I hoped was that I would be offered a severance package. I had actually previously made a pact with God, that if this was ever offered to me, I would take it, and then metaphorically jump off the cliff and fully in to my new existence as The Message Architect. And lo and behold, that's precisely what happened! The stars were aligning for me.

And here's the really cool part. Soon after I signed the offer to take the severance package, I hopped on a flight to moderate a highly regarded presidential event – in Dubai! I was finally going global! From the minute I set foot in Dubai, I knew there was absolutely no limit to where my The Message Architect journey would take me, and I felt the limitations of being restricted to my birth country alone being lifted. I was able to experience that event with my country watching me represent them on live television, as it was broadcast, and with the full support of the global presidents and ministers who were present.

I learned in that experience that it does not matter how many people are watching you, it is about the quality of the people watching – so stop worrying about the number of likes and views you get on social media, and rather focus on that one like that has the potential to change your life. (This is a lesson I still have to remind myself of when the pressures of society want to choke me.)

On the flight back home from Dubai, I watched a movie that gave me some thoughts about something that would stick with me for many years to come. The movie was *King Richard*, about tennis superstars Venus and Serena Williams, and their father. They themselves are bestselling books, if we view lives as novels or storylines.

When the movie finished, I jotted down these notes: 'It is in stories like these that I am constantly reminded by my fellow winners who I am. We come from families and loved ones that have poured energy into us and fuelled our fires in many different ways, and so when we win, it is not only for ourselves but for the hope we feel responsible to give everyone else. My future, too, was secured through love, consistent support and damned hard work, so when I work hard and I get the spotlight, it is not only for me, it is for the representation I am accountable to; it is also for the ones who resonate with where I am from and who I am: an African, a dreamer, a fighter, an experience. Everything from here on is for us. Our dreams are valid. My African voice to the globe.'

It was then that I realised that my life story was always going to be a bestselling book in the library of life. I might have been the book at the back of the shelf, with dust all over it, and only a third written, but it was just waiting for me to pick it up and fill in the remaining blank pages.

I do not know how you view your life, but if you were made with intentionality, you have to be a bestselling book in life's library. Every book is uniquely written; every book has a lesson to teach, a story to tell, if you just allow it.

Live your life to the fullest, because the best books are the ones filled with stories that keep you glued to the pages. All you have to decide is whether your bestselling book will be a horror, a comedy, a thriller or even a romance. I have chosen to make my story poetic.

> Give yourself permission to be experienced truthfully by others. You are a once-in-a-lifetime encounter.

12

Uncover the journey of your destiny

People often speak about reaching a crossroads in their lives. This is where and when decisions are meant to be made, and often they are difficult decisions.

I suppose, given the fact that life is really made up of a bunch of decisions, from the time you can crawl until your last day, the emphasis on decision-making cannot be spotlighted enough.

What we perhaps do not talk about enough is the speed limit in life on these roads. Just as on the actual streets we travel on each day, some have a higher speed limit than others. Some are highways and can be experienced quickly, while others are quiet avenues in neighbourhoods where slow and careful driving is preferred.

Because we are always discovering and navigating through life, path choices are always going to be present. We can never know how the paths may unfold; they develop as you make choices. This means that every decision you make will reveal a different path.

I do believe that regardless of the paths you take, they will always take you to a series of crossroads, where you are given a chance to either remain on the road you're on, or continue on another. I am not sure how many crossroads we are given in a life span but I am certain it is more than one; in my case, life has gifted me a number of these, and I'm certain there will be more going forward.

Some paths unfold rather effortlessly and rapidly, while others take time to reveal themselves. I will let you into a beautiful part of my life in which a path was revealed super-slowly, but was one that led to a massive crossroads in my life.

Before Tony and I became a couple, I had actually known him for almost a decade. Never in my wildest dreams did I ever think he would be the one. I first met him at the Elangeni Hotel in Durban. I was there to attend a conference in the tourism sector, representing the company I was working for at the time.

I was super-excited: to be selected for travel in our jobs and workplaces is a big deal. I was growing in my career to a point that I was being chosen due to my work ethic and contribution to the business. I wanted to continue to knuckle down and focus on growing in that career, and that was all that was in my mind. Meeting a man was the least of my expectations.

Tony was also attending the conference as a representative in the tourism sector. Although Tony and I were both born in Gauteng, and I was still based there, he had just left that province to move fulltime to KwaZulu-Natal. (Now, we both also call KwaZulu-Natal home, because we've spent some special years and moments there.)

Tony spotted me before I noticed him. I think he spotted me because he had been in the industry for a while, and most of the other faces had become familiar to him over time, and he picked up on the fact that he had not seen my face before. We laughed about it years later when he admitted that from the time he laid eyes on me, he was drawn to me, and from the time we spoke, he knew he wanted me to be his wife one day. I have always heard that men have some sort of sixth sense when it comes to this. If they do not, then this was sheer will on Tony's part!

On that day, the conference, Tony didn't approach me; he just watched me from a distance. But at lunch time he made absolutely sure that he was standing next to me in the buffet queue.

As we neared the table to begin dishing up lunch for ourselves, he started a conversation with me. He told me afterwards that he figured that if we were in mid-conversation by the time we'd filled our plates, he could naturally ask me if he could join me at my table and eat with me.

Our conversation started off with general questions, and we quickly established that my boss at the time was a dear varsity friend of his. Nothing is ever coincidence, and I will continue to preach this!

The smartest move was when he chose a table that seated only two – this guy was clearly on a mission! He didn't ask if I had a partner but I made sure that he was well aware of it (I was dating Owen at the time), so I could quickly shut down any unnecessary banter along that trajectory. I could tell that he was bummed that I was already spoken for. Still, he was a complete gentleman.

A few days later I received a call from my manager. She was quite giggly and said she wasn't sure how to approach the conversation, but that an old university friend of hers had just called her and asked for my phone number – she was calling to ask permission from me to give it to him. I knew she was talking about Tony. She explained that he had told her that we'd had lunch together at the conference, and that he'd forgotten to take my number. He had not forgotten – he just knew that I would not have given it to him!

I agreed that she could share my phone number with him. I had seen absolutely no potential in Tony being a threat to my relationship – and even if he did attempt to pursue me, I saw no harm in making a new connection.

Over the next few years, Tony would check in on me occasionally. He always initiated the calls, and I would forget that he existed after the conversations were done each time. We would talk about the most ridiculous and general stuff. He followed me on social media, and I still laugh at some of the comments he made back then on my posts: he was light-hearted and genuine.

During the course of Tony's and my friendship, I got married to Owen, and Tony continued to date other women. We were not shy to share details of our love lives because we were really building a solid friendship.

Tony really was an eligible bachelor during the time we were building a friendship and he knew it, but his heart knew what he was looking for and he was not going to settle. He would have rather gone through life a single guy than settle, I admire that about him.

In his 'stalking' of me on social media – please note that Tony and I tease each other ridiculously, and that is the nature of our friendship – he noticed that there were fewer and fewer pictures of me with Owen, but he would never pick up the phone and blatantly ask me about it; and even if he had, I would have not answered genuinely because it was a difficult situation I was going through.

He and I were growing closer in many ways but he still showed no indication that he fancied me. I actually used to ask him if I could help him find a partner who would be suitable for him, and he would describe his ideal girl to me. The description of this ideal girl sounded a lot like me, and in fact he sometimes even said, 'I want a girl just like you,' but those words completely flew over my head. I was excited that he wanted someone like me, because I knew that when I found a kindred spirit, I could introduce them to each other. Not once did I think he was hinting. I just wanted him to be happy. His happiness has always mattered to me, and always will.

Interestingly, during those years of friendship, he would diss all my partners. He would tell me how they needed to fix themselves and needed to find their ideal partner because I was not it!

A little over a year after my divorce, I got a message from him: 'Hey, I am in Gauteng.' I remember being confused and irritated by it, because I was not sure what he expected me to do with this piece of information. The last time I had physically seen Tony was a few years prior, at a conference. I had never hung out with him for any significant periods of time – our friendship right up until that message consisted of phone calls coupled with haphazard meetings at conferences, and that was it.

I did, however, agree to have lunch with him the next day. We agreed to meet at Papachinos in Midrand. He had arrived before me, and he spotted me getting out of my car. When we saw each other, our hug did last longer than a normal friendly hug but we never spoke of it on that day. (He was smelling super-delicious, so I hung on!)

Not only does Tony always smell great, I could tell from very early on that he was super-clean and tidy by the way he dressed. I used to wonder if he ever had anything out of place at his house. There is neat and clean, and then there is Tony. Our mom (his biological mother) told me a story that he used to wear white clothes as a young boy, and he would be the only child to come back spotless, without a sign or trace of dirt. This cleanliness has worked in my favour in our marriage and home, as he is still super-clean and I am extremely tidy.

Anyway, I'd told him I could only stay for an hour for the lunch (in case things didn't work out and I wanted to leave) but we landed up staying at Papachinos for almost four hours. During our conversations over our meal, I made it quite clear that men had hurt me and I was not looking for a relationship, so he would just need to continue being my friend and nothing else. He nodded but apparently his heart did not agree.

Three weeks after that lunch, we began dating. I flew to Durban for my birthday, and when I met him at the airport, it was as if a cloth had been lifted from my eyes. He looked so fine! He had never looked fine to me before; to me, he was just a guy. Giggling, I asked him if he had always looked the way he did to me on that day. I was finally seeing him with different eyes.

Tony and I dated for just three months before we got engaged – we had been a part of each other's lives for years, so there was no reason to wait. For me, Tony felt safe to be around. He felt like peace to me, like home.

We got married eight months later.

I knew I had to proceed with lobola proceedings to appease the families, but our lobola was unconventional. Tony was all too happy to go the unconventional route to accommodate me and to make it less stressful on me. I agreed to a once-off meeting, and the amount to be requested was pre-agreed, so we did not have to go back and forth. Straight after that single meeting, we went into the western part of the wedding (very simple, held in a garden). This means I technically still owe my husband a traditional wedding!

Tony knew from the day he met me that I was the one, and he was correct. He had long unfolded that path before I had. I am so glad that when Tony reached his crossroads where one of the roads led to me, he came off his path to find me on mine and guide me along it.

When they say you should marry your friend, please do yourself a favour and listen to this advice! It is the best thing I could have ever done for myself in this lifetime.

In marrying Tony, I scored and won big time. He is incredibly smart, he is honest, he is super-kind, he is considerate, he loves genuinely and deeply, and he listens to both spoken and unspoken words like a charm. You could easily assume that you are Tony's friend after one engagement with him.

He used to tell me, after I'd unpacked my history to him, that he would not be going anywhere, and that he would be here for it all, and after years of being friends, I believe him. He was certain that he would not leave me because of my unsuccessful relationships in the past, and neither would he leave because of my abandonment issues. I am without doubt that he is deliberately ensuring that his path is parallel to mine. He is the first and only adult man in my life to show me what untainted, true love is, and I am thankful that he has taken his time to peel the love onion that I am, and find the hidden heart. He has been a standout teacher to me in many ways.

I have told Tony he cannot leave me because I refuse to go through another divorce, and I do not possess the vocabulary to explain any of that to the children. I am on my third surname in life, and this is the one I am sticking with! Whether he likes it or not, he is stuck with me – but I am confident that he *does* like it; he is happily stuck with me.

I now believe that love was unkind to me up until the crossroads with Tony for a reason: sometimes we have to experience the dark to appreciate the light. Had I not faced what I had faced, I am not sure I would appreciate him. I think I would have possibly taken advantage of his patience, kindness and willingness to help me fully – but I do not do any of that, because I know what it's like to have partners who are impatient, unkind and selfish.

This has made me realise that when we say people have a purpose, we almost always assume that purpose is something positive. However, in reality, some people have a purpose to cause pain, trauma and drama in your life, so that you can draw from that, and reflect on and appreciate what comes in your future. The objective of some relationships is solely to teach you lessons, and not to journey with you, and those lessons can be a double-edged sword.

We are currently in a beautiful space, Tony and I. I love my husband so deeply, but marriage is not a magic wand that miraculously turns life into a full-time 'holidays and movie nights' bed of roses. Marriage takes effort, it takes contribution; it is choosing each other when the ugly sides of you are rearing their ugly heads at each other.

Tony is calm; I am not. He is observant; I am not. He is a night person, I am a morning person. And so the see-saw goes. But he is in every way my best friend, and the one person I am certain has my back through and through. No matter where the paths go, he is always my pit stop, my resting place, my refilling station.

No matter where the paths of life take you, remember to be very vigilant and observant, because the crossroads are sure to come, and there are many of them. Be alert and patient – but at the same time, enjoy the journey, the run, the ride on the paths of your life.

Life is filled with choices but you must enjoy each and every aspect in between too – that is the entire point of living!

> Every path has a destination, no matter how long it takes you to get there.

13

Give and take

We are all uniquely made, and we are all intentionally made. Intention means we have something we need to fulfil, to achieve.

The world is full of give and take: we take from others what we cannot provide for ourselves, and others take from us in the same manner. Even love can be a demand you make of those who care for you. 'Demand' may sound like a strong word, but all it means is that there is a need, desire or wish from one person for them to feel content and satisfied; it may not necessarily be demanded aggressively. I believe that we all have inner desires and needs that must be met for us to even begin to walk through life in a purely pleasant way.

In the same way as we all have these needs, we are also the supply to others' demands, through matters such as love, care and help for the next person in your life. It is not something we can escape – it is the circle and the very nature of life.

Further to this emotional demand you fulfil, there are other areas in which you provide for demands through your various roles, including those in your career. You are always in demand – you just need to explore why, and once you discover that, the rest will start to make more sense.

My journey to discovering why I am in demand has been fun. Most of it I only understand in hindsight but I am thankful there was a specific period when I unpacked it.

If you are uncertain why you are in demand, start by acknowledging that you simply *are*, and then start finding moments that begin to reveal the significance of your demand. When did you feel as though you were needed by others and you were able to deliver on that need?

Once I had discovered why I am in demand – and, trust me, we are *all* in demand in some way or another – I made it my business to continue reminding myself constantly through forms of mantras. A mantra is simply a statement or a slogan that you repeat often.

My mantras remind me that I am not just floating through life, that I actually was created with intention. I have a handful of my mantras that are my secrets to guide me through life but I will share the one that I started to build on as I fully immersed myself in my calling: I, Thami Nkadimeng, I am blessed to bless!

Finding a declaration/s or mantra/s that you want to live by will keep you focused on what you are building in your continuous scripting of life. Find yours and it will be your guiding light in good times, but also and especially in times of doubt or difficulty.

Learning to be strong – to be an assertive woman – has been a road indeed for me. That road has had both tarred and gravel surfaces, as well as the sharpest turns and, at times, the smoothest lines. It is a road that has given me perspective.

Until I became The Message Architect, I always thought I wanted a seamless life that would see me reaching the right milestones at the right time: go to school, go to university, find a boyfriend, build my career, get married and then have children. This is in no way what the universe dealt me, and I am just fine with that. The universe gave me an opportunity to break the template of a 'perfect life' in many ways, and for this I am beyond thankful.

When I got my first job, it was because I wanted to provide; and because of that, I started building my career quite quickly. That alone was something that threw me off the customary options. And I can tell you for free, I am now internally richer for having had things work out from mains to starter to dessert. I worked, became a mom, then married, then started building the career I was always meant to be in. Having had it go this way has enabled me to enjoy the wins like sacred jewels. I often remind myself, for example, how I had to juggle studying while nursing a child, and the motivation I got from that.

I have had to build through tough times. If my life could be described as a house, having a house that remains standing strong is not as easy as buying a piece of land, drawing up plans, building the house, then furnishing it. Some parts of my house have been built with rocks, others with bricks, and some even with cow dung – but the house is standing proud because the foundation is solid. It all worked out, and I believe it will continue to work in my favour because everything about me and my life is intentional.

I may no longer go to shops with so little money in my purse that I have to choose between necessities, but I am still a stickler for budgets and fanatical about sticking to them. I know that being able to buy things without worrying about where the next rand is coming from is a privilege: having been in the dark has helped me to see the light.

Being able to earn is a liberty I have had to grow into; having funds liberates you from having to ask others for money. I used to save up the money and not spend any on myself at all, because of the 'what ifs'. I started to resent having to work to earn a living, because my relationship with money was tainted by my having grown up with bursts of lack and bursts of sufficiency. I felt that if I filled up my pockets, I could possibly rid myself of lack and fill the emotional need. Not true! Enjoy the money, but enjoy it wisely; and I choose to enjoy it privately too, because it is a blessing.

I have found that staying humble can mean you are overlooked in a world full of 'look at me' syndrome – but this is only ever for a short period of time, because in the end you win at what you are meant to win at, and you also lose when you are meant to lose.

It took me until I was thirty-four years old, in 2019, to stop apologising for being talented at what I do, and stop asking for imaginary permission to chase my life calling. That year, I adopted a phrase: 'Sorry Not Sorry'. It was sparked and motivated by both Rachel Hollis's book published that year, *Girl, Stop Apologizing*, and a 2017 Demi Lovato song.

In the book, subtitled *A Shame-Free Plan for Embracing and Achieving Your Goals*, Hollis, a bestselling author and founder of a multimillion-dollar media company, points out that many women have been taught to define themselves in light of other people, whether as wife, mother, daughter or employee, instead of learning how to own who they are and what they want.

In the song 'Sorry Not Sorry', Lovato sings about 'feeling inspired 'cause the tables have turned / Yeah, I'm on fire and I know that it burns'. Well, that's how I feel: I am here and I am going to be bold about being here, because the world will never get another chance to experience Thami Nkadimeng once my time is up when I reach my nineties, so making a mark and an impact is no longer an option.

I am the Almighty's deliverable; and if I am His deliverable, it means I am also His KPI – His key performance indicator – and His portfolio of evidence. I do not think He gets anything less that 10 out of 5 in His work. I do not want to be the tool that steered Him to achieving anything less than excellence.

I encourage you to find your own unique drive and let it inspire you to be more than average, to be a benchmark, to be an experience to humankind – to be excellent.

American meteorologist Stephen Corfidi, a person with extraordinary forecasting skills, writes that the main reason the sky puts on such a show after a storm is because clean air is the perfect ingredient for brightly coloured sunrises and sunsets. I have faced my thunderstorms, and now I am happy to display my rainbows: to demonstrate my teachings through my work, my personality and experiences thus far. My journey is far from over but if I look at the weather forecast of my life, I believe it is going to be mostly sunny, with a few showers here and there, rather than thunderstorms all the way through.

Over the years, I have come to look at the meaning of all the many elements in my life together, and I have realised that I have always been on the winning side when I was willing to learn. I have come to realise that if you ask yourself the right questions, no matter what your circumstances, you will recognise that you are on the winning side if you choose to be.

I use the acronym 'hungry' to evaluate whether I'm effectively honouring myself and my drive for a changed life in comparison to my childhood. In order to remain hungry for a better tomorrow and a future of which I can be proud, I ask myself a series of questions under a key word for each letter. These questions have certainly helped me and I hope they help you too.

Honour

- Are you constantly honouring yourself in the choices you're making?
- Are you honouring your previous life lessons, or were they all just events?
- Are you choosing yourself consistently, while considering others, and not the other way around?

Undo

- Are you undoing your past mistakes, even if it is bit by bit?
- Are you undoing telling yourself that you're not worthy of a great life because of your history?

- Are you choosing to create a better life for future generations by undoing what was created before?

Now

- Are you understanding that you are needed by society to make your mark now, not only when you are perfect?
- Are you understanding that if you do not use now to make a difference, you will have lost that now and will never get it back?
- Do you understand that you were born at a specific time and date for a reason: because it is when you are required?

Great

- Are you giving your 'good' or your 'great' to the life you're living?
- Are you striving to leave greatness as a legacy?
- Do you acknowledge that you were born not average, but great?

Repeat

- Are you repeating the healthy and positive patterns of life you have accumulated to make that your new reality?
- Are you repeatedly telling yourself that your history is not who you are but what has happened to you?

- Are you consistently and repeatedly chasing the true version of yourself, because with that comes the best of you?

You
- Are you acknowledging that the accountability of your life remains with you?
- Are you aware that there is only one you?
- Are you aware that certain scenarios would not be complete without you: only you can make certain things whole?

I am not perfect, and I do not ever want to be perfect, because that would mean I have nothing further to learn. I want life to keep teaching me, but I also ask for the teaching to be a lot kinder than what I experienced in my first three decades of life! I want to continue scripting and rehearsing, to continue performing and to continue reviewing, because that is the only way to confidently say that I honestly gave it my best shot to live, and not just to exist.

I consider myself a walking miracle and will continue to live my life as such. I am comfortable in my own skin! I am no longer winging it. I am fulfilling what I was told to fulfil since I was a young girl in my room pretending there is a crowd watching me and introducing myself to them.

I was given this life to share as a lesson and I will continue to do so. Feel free to choose and share the parts of my life story that could help you, your children, your parents, your colleagues – because my life has been and will be a buffet to be enjoyed.

I was the right character in the wrong play, and now I have changed not just the play's script but the theatre too, to achieve what I am meant to. I am not lucky; I am loved and I am building something.

I wish you deep self-discovery. I wish you reflection. And I wish you upcoming realisation and gratification in all you do.

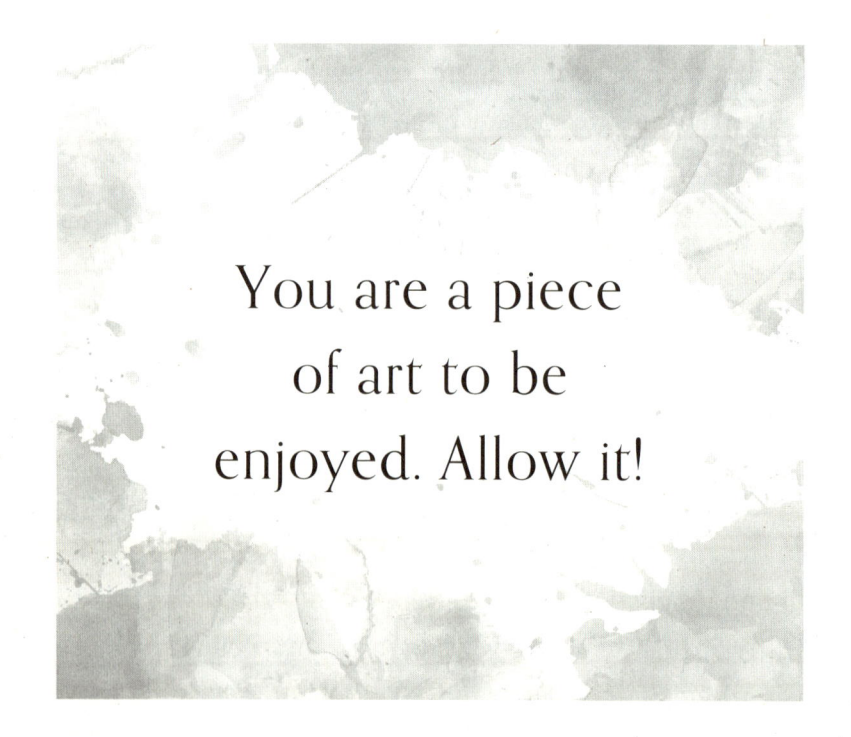

> You are a piece of art to be enjoyed. Allow it!

Conclusion

I sometimes choose to look at life like a casino of sorts. For those who have never been to a casino, allow me to paint a picture for you and transport your imagination to this place that can either work in your favour or not – but the trick is to have fun either way.

Imagine gaming tables, slot machines, the constant sound of bells ringing and people talking, and hope floating around in the air – all this in a room filled with anticipation, and with hints of victory, but also with the smell of desperation in some corners.

There is nothing wrong with a casino in and of itself. However, 'addiction' is a connotation closely linked to the word 'casino'. This is based on people taking their money, sometimes even their life savings, in the hope of multiplying that money and, by pure luck, striking it rich. Because they get little wins – a few hundred rands here, and maybe even a few thousand there – the downfall occurs when people become addicted to the feeling of promised wins without calculating risks.

Life can be like this: you have to calculate the risks and the possibility of losing against the balance of fun. You – and all of us – also have to understand that there is no such thing as winning all the time. But, luckily, this applies in reverse too: there is no such thing as losing all the time either. It is quite the relief that balance exists in life!

I like to think of it as every win has a loss, even if their weights are not equal. You have to calculate your risks with each hand dealt to you by life. Also, unlike an actual deck of cards, your life cards can change with every situation. And I believe that we are each dealt a bonus 'get out of the situation free' card. You need to take time to figure out which card this is to you. For me, it's the joker.

You, like me, are a creator – you just need to become conscious of what it is you are creating. You are a gift to this world, its history and its future, in one way or the other.

With this in mind, remember that not all gifts are pleasant. I'm sure we have all received a gift at some point that we showed appreciation for when we got it, but never looked at again; some have received a gift and regifted it to someone else because we did not want it. So, ask yourself: are you going to be a good gift to this world? I choose to be a good gift to the world.

May we all reflect and remember that we are not haphazard ideas. We are made with intention, and because of this, we must continue to dream, and dream big, and to reflect on our life mistakes and joys as lessons.

The only thing standing between the idea of your dreams and you realising them is the depth of your commitment to them, regardless of the situations thrown at you.

Acknowledgements

I want to start by thanking my Creator for choosing this incredibly fulfilling life for me.

It goes without saying that my mother played a starring role in all of this, from the time she decided to carry me in her womb to now being my girlfriend – thanks, Jo!

To my three boys, thanks for being there for me as I navigate my pursuit, with such grace, love and tons of tolerance.

To my squad – thanks for helping to pick it all up when it falls apart at times.

To Lincoln Mali – you rock, brother!

To my publisher and the team involved – thanks for believing in me.

To my inner self – Thami, thanks for navigating life when I have no clue where we are heading, I trust you with everything within me.

To all my supporters on social media and on other platforms – thank you!

And to you, my readers – thank you too! I am because you encourage me to be.

About the author

Photographer: Benedict Jimu

Thami Nkadimeng is The Message Architect. She uses her background in communications to make positive change and contribute to a harmonious society for all. With a passion for untangling complex and intricate topics through conversation, she influences positive change towards a better world and contributes towards the United Nations Sustainability Goals of narrowing social disparities in a provoking, directed, motivated and effective manner. She advocates being the example of change you want to see in the world as individuals.

Thami holds an undergraduate degree in communications science, a diploma (cum laude) in marketing management and an honours degree in integrated organisational communication. She has worked, and continues to work, with presidents, leaders, executives, corporates and organisations worldwide. In 2023 she was named on the '100 Under 40' list of the Most Influential People of African Descent (MIPAD) in support of the International Decade for People of African Descent proclaimed by the United Nations' General Assembly to be observed from 2015 to 2024.

Thami lives in Johannesburg with her husband and two sons.